"*My Father Was a Gangster: The Jim Vaus Stor*[...] tive of one of the most colorful, most comp[...] characters of recent times. Written by his son, Will, the book vividly illustrates how the transforming power of faith in Christ can dramatically change the life of the most seasoned criminal. The reader will find it difficult to put the book down."

> DR. ARMAND M. NICHOLI, JR.
> Professor of Psychiatry, Harvard Medical School
> Author of *The Question of God*

"The story of Jim Vaus needs to be read and shared by this generation. He is a tremendous example of a man who had a dramatic encounter with the living God and whose story has impacted countless lives. Take time to read it, absorb it, and share it."

> STEVE RUSSO
> International speaker and best-selling author
> Host of the syndicated daily radio program *Real Answers*

"I first heard of Jim Vaus shortly after Billy Graham's first Los Angeles Crusade in 1949. It was therefore quite remarkable that I was the one to be selected to organize a program for him in the British Isles. At the time I was working with the British Evangelical Alliance, and my friend George Wilson (who had been business manager at Northwestern College when I was there in 1948/9) had asked me to do this.

"We had a remarkable time with Jim and his wife as we took them to church after church where, time and again, he told the story of his conversion. More importantly (for me) he brought with him one of the tiny 'bugging' microphones, which he had removed from Mickey Cohen's house, and when he left England, he left it with me. I still have it - and it is a prized possession.

"To me it seemed inevitable that Jim would devote his life to Christian service—and so it was. It was not long before I heard the story of what he was doing and, as a result, he remained on my prayer list for the rest of his life.

"God has many trophies as He works through the proclamation of His word. Through the ministry of Billy Graham in the Los Angeles

tent, Jim was one of them. Surely his welcome into heaven must have been accompanied by the angel choir singing 'Well done, good and faithful servant. Enter into the joy of your Lord!'"

MAURICE ROWLANDSON
April 2007
Author of *Behind the Scenes with Billy Graham* and *Life on Water*

"*My Father Was a Gangster: The Jim Vaus Story* is a powerful reminder of how God reaches into the lives of the most unlikely people, redeems them from a destructive way of life and makes them powerful instruments of His Gospel in ministry. It is refreshing to see the story told again by Will Vaus, Jim's son.

I remember well the first biography and the subsequent movie, *The Wiretapper*. As it touched my life then, so I trust this story will touch many lives today."

JOHN GUEST
Senior Pastor, Christ Church at Grove Farm
Pittsburgh, Pennsylvania

I am delighted that there is a new book about Jim Vaus as his echoing story deserves this generation's full attention. The time I spent with Jim was short but its effect on my life will be long lasting. I first met him when he spoke to a group of Christians active in the business of New York City Theater. He was a champion of Godly newness. His ministry would shake up the world's indifference at the tawdriness of misguided young people and offer instead the surprising validity of hope.

I returned to Houston to work as an actress in the Alley Theater and started a small group Bible study within Houston's theater community. I asked Jim to come to Houston to speak to a gathering of that group in my home and invited a few guests. Jim's name and the impact of his work brought a crowd to my house that immediately out distanced the amount of food I had prepared. Jim joined me in the kitchen and laughed at my dilemma as I divided the considered portions and literally watered the cups of soup. My living room was crowded and no comfortable chair was left for our guest of honor. He perched awkwardly on the arm of an undersized sofa and spoke to a

wide-eyed group of underfed guests who never noticed the scant service in the wonderment of Jim's abundant words. Later I realized how appropriate that evening was. Jim was seldom confined within the expectations of the ordinary and much of his work was spent in undersized accommodations serving those whom society had underfed. God had a special place for Jim. No other ministry served as Jim's did and in a manner seldom equaled, Jim did not require agreement or fellowship; with or without it...he served in obedience to God...and that ministering service had and still has performance.

Many years have passed since that season of my life. I have become the Artistic Director of a Christian Theater that began at a time when I knew no similar ministry offering the pattern of fellowship and scant recognition of its purpose. Now, in our 40[th] season I see my work as an outcropping of what I learned from Jim: when God calls unto a new ministry we dare not wait for the future to catch up with us. God had a word for Jim: authenticity. Jim was authentic in his faith, authentic in his friendship, authentic in his love for his family, authentic in his humor, authentic in his sorrows and authentic in his joy. That authenticity defined his ministry and reflected the One absolute God in Whom we can trust absolutely.

JEANNETTE CLIFT GEORGE
Founder & Artistic Director
A.D. Players
Houston, Texas

Jim Vaus' story of crime and salvation is a glorious testimony to the redemptive power of Christ. As told by his son Will, Jim's journey from rebellious youth to wiretapper to servant of God seems a drama straight from a Hollywood script. Jim Vaus left a legacy of service to his Lord and love for his family that is both compelling and inspiring.

LUIS PALAU,
President, Luis Palau Association

MY
FATHER
WAS A
GANGSTER

MY FATHER WAS A GANGSTER

The Jim Vaus Story

Will Vaus

BELIEVE BOOKS
Life Stories That Inspire
WASHINGTON, DC

MY FATHER WAS A GANGSTER
By Will Vaus

Unless otherwise noted, all Scripture quotations are from the HOLY BIBLE, KING JAMES VERSION (KJV).

Scripture quotations identified as NLT are taken from the Holy Bible, New Living Translation, copyright 1996, 2004. Used by permission of Tyndale House Publishers, Inc., Wheaton, Illinois 60189. All rights reserved.

Scripture quotations identified as NIV are taken from the HOLY BIBLE, NEW INTERNATIONAL VERSION ®. Copyright © 1973, 1978, 1984 International Bible Society. Used by permission of Zondervan. All rights reserved.

"NIV" and "NEW INTERNATIONAL VERSION" are trademarks registered in the United States Patent and Trademark Office by International Bible Society ®. Use of either trademark requires the permission of International Bible Society.

Cover photo used by permission, © AP Images 1958.

Excerpt from *Our Littlest Angel* by Mrs. Jim Vaus © 1962 Mrs. Jim Vaus. Extract reprinted by permission.

Excerpts from *The Devil Loves a Shining Mark* by Jim Vaus with Julie Maxey © Word Incorporated. 1974. Extracts reprinted without quotation marks by permission of The Jim Vaus Estate and Julie Maxey.

Excerpts from *They Called My Husband a Gangster* by Mrs. Jim (Alice) Vaus as told to Dorothy C. Haskin © Van Kampen Press, Inc. 1952. Extracts reprinted without quotation marks by permission of Alice Vaus.

Excerpts from *Why I Quit Syndicated Crime* by Jim Vaus as told to D. C. Haskin © Van Kampen Press, Inc. 1951. Extracts reprinted without quotation marks by permission of The Jim Vaus Estate.

ISBN: 0-9787428-2-6

Library of Congress Control Number: 2007935124

Cover design: *Jack Kotowicz, Washington, DC, VelocityDesignGroup.com*
Layout design: *Annie Kotowicz*

Believe Books publishes the inspirational life stories of extraordinary believers in God from around the world. Requests for information should be addressed to **Believe Books** at www.believebooks.com. **Believe Books** is a registered trade name of **Believe Books, LLC** of Washington, DC.

Printed in the United States of America

For Mom,
the unsung hero of this story.
Love always ...

CONTENTS

Part Three: Filling Others' Emptiness (1958-1970)

Part Four: Overflowing (1971-1997)

FOREWORD

It was the fall of 1949 when I first heard the name of Jim Vaus. That September I had enrolled at Wheaton College at the recommendation of Billy Graham who had spoken at a youth rally that I was leading and told me about his alma mater.

One of the first Sundays at college I went eagerly with friends to hear Billy preach at the church he pastored in Western Springs, Illinois. That Sunday night he left for Los Angeles to begin the evangelistic campaign that would make him first a local, then a national, then an internationally-known evangelist.

The headlines of his extended preaching in Los Angeles excited me and the other young aspiring preachers at Wheaton. We were intrigued not just at the crowds, but the "name" figures who gave their lives to Christ then—the cowboy singer Stuart Hamblen, the Olympic runner and war hero Lou Zamperini, and, most unusual of all, a wiretapper for the gangster Mickey Cohen named Jim Vaus.

Jim was only the name of a kind of "celebrity" then. Later I came to know him as he became a man of God, a lover of young people, a devoted father, a man marked by God's grace.

Sometimes one who has been dramatically converted is described as a "trophy of grace." Does that conjure up the image of a glass-covered cabinet in heaven where Jesus proudly displays the "trophies" he has won? Hardly.

What matters to the Lord (and should to us) is when someone who has come to faith in Christ, famous or ordinary, becomes a "letter from Christ", to use Paul's metaphor—one in whom the marks of Christ are seen.

Jim Vaus, as I came to know him, was such a "letter."

He was a good-sized letter, a big, towering giant of a man who also exuded the loving gentleness of his Lord.

He was a fun-loving letter. My wife Jeanie and I learned how he loved practical jokes when at our wedding (where her brother Billy officiated) Jim hinted that as a reformed wiretapper, he was going to use his skills to "bug" our honeymoon hotel!

Most of all, he was a God-loving and people-loving letter. After his conversion Jim became a kind of evangelical "celebrity", traveling from city to city to give his testimony. But that was not enough.

He became a letter from Christ to gang members in the heart of New York City, moving into the ghetto to reach hard-core youngsters, sharing with them in word and deed and presence the love of Christ that had changed his life.

And Jim was a long-lasting letter to those in his family who knew him best. His son Will was also called to ministry, and it was my joy to have Will associated for a time with our own ministry of evangelism and leadership training. Will is a second-generation letter from Christ.

So Jim was, and is still, in heaven—a letter worth God's writing. And this book is worth your reading. It is a story that needs to be told, remembered, and one that leads us to praise the God of grace who met Jim Vaus in that canvas cathedral in Los Angeles, and is still ready to enter and transform lives today.

LEIGHTON FORD
President, Leighton Ford Ministries
Charlotte, North Carolina

ACKNOWLEDGEMENTS

First of all, my gratitude goes to my publisher, Believe Books. True to the name of their company, they believed in this book enough to bring it to publication and their assistance in the editing process was invaluable.

I might not have embarked on this project were it not for the encouragement of James Howdyshell, who took particular interest in my father's life story and wanted to see a book about him in print. That encouragement sent me on a journey through notes my father had compiled about his life in preparation for a new autobiography he hoped to publish. Unfortunately, that project was postponed by his death, but is now brought to completion here. This project also forced me to sort through literally boxes upon boxes of photographs chronicling my father's unusual life. I deeply appreciate the assistance of Jack Flynn in helping me scan the photographs to be included in this book.

I could not have written this work as completely as I have without recourse to three previous biographical works about my parents: *Why I Quit Syndicated Crime*, written by my father with the assistance of Dorothy C. Haskin; *They Called My Husband a Gangster*, written by my mother also with the assistance of Dorothy Haskin; and *The Devil Loves a Shining Mark*, written by my father with the help of Julie Maxey.

This book would also not have come to be without the help of my mother, Alice Vaus, who consented to long interviews and who sat through a seemingly endless reading aloud of the first draft. We relived many family moments, not without many tears and much laughter, as we worked on this book together.

Thanks are also due to my brother Steve, whose earlier, unpublished manuscript on my father's life refreshed my memory on many key points. I am indebted to him for a number of valuable comments on the first draft of this book.

I am also deeply appreciative of the input I received from my father's two sisters, Elizabeth Rothenberger and Virginia McLaughlin. I enjoyed many good telephone calls talking to both of these wonderful aunts in the process of writing about their much-loved brother.

Thanks too are due to Betty Craig, my father's secretary for forty years. Without her meticulous attention to detailed archiving, many of the sources of information upon which this book is based would have been lost to future generations.

While I hope this book will be of benefit to many people around the world, one of my greatest desires is that this story will serve as a lasting legacy for my children to remind them often of what an amazing grandfather they had and how powerful and loving our God really is. Thanks to my wife Becky, and to each of my sons, James, Jonathan and Joshua, for allowing me the time to bring this project to fruition.

Finally, my greatest debt belongs to the God who called first my father, and then me, to himself through Jesus Christ. To God be all the glory.

PROLOGUE

The first time I realized my father, Jim Vaus, had done anything of note was the day, sometime in the late 1960's, when he was to be interviewed on the *Today Show* by Barbara Walters. As things turned out, his interview was broadcast during the last half hour of the program and I had to catch the elementary school bus at 8:30 a.m. I pleaded with my mother to let me stay home and watch the show, but my mother had her priorities, and getting me to school on time rated higher than letting me watch my father on a nationally televised news program.

I knew my father was the executive director of an organization, Youth Development, Inc., seeking to help youth in inner-city New York. We had spent our summers at Camp Champion in upstate New York—a camp Dad had started for the kids from Harlem. I can even recall touring some of the facilities run by YDI in the area of Hell Gate Station, NYC. But for the most part, all I knew of my father's work centered around his offices in Tarrytown on the Hudson where we also made our home. The Tarrytown office was filled with computer equipment occupying entire rooms, and it was also the abode of secretaries who treated me like a miniature visiting dignitary whenever I dropped by.

I usually had a difficult time in school describing what my father did for work. Other kids' dads were doctors or lawyers or engineers. What did my dad do? I could never tell, until I learned the word entrepreneur; when others heard a kid use that word they didn't ask any more questions.

The next inkling I got of my father's unusual life came to me after our family moved from Tarrytown, New York to San Diego, California in January of 1971. In 1972, a friend of my father got out of jail after a long prison sentence. His name was Mickey Cohen. We saw a lot of Mickey from 1972 until 1976, when he died of cancer. I believe my parents watched *The Godfather* with Mickey at a movie theater somewhere. That had to be interesting, since a good part of the movie was based upon Mickey's life; even Marlon Brando's husky voice was typical of Mickey.

There were also visits to Chasen's Restaurant, a glamorous hangout for movie stars in Beverly Hills, and we socialized with Cohen and his cronies at his apartment in Westwood. Mickey even spent the day with us on our boat out on the Pacific Ocean, bringing along his then current female companion, actress Lita Baron.

However, the thing that stands out most in my memory is the evening Cohen spent with us in our home as we watched a movie on 16mm, a motion picture I had never heard of before. The film was called *The Wiretapper* and it was the story of my dad's life in organized crime, when he used to work for Cohen back in the late 1940's. It was an eye-opener for me at ten years of age. But for my parents, it was almost like watching a home movie. My dad always thought the acting was corny, or "corn-ball" as he used to say. But for Mickey this was a serious event. He had to keep telling my mom, "Dummy up Alice!" through the whole movie because she was talking and laughing too much as we watched.

People often ask me, "So your father never sat down and explained to you that he had once been involved in organized crime?"

My answer: "No, my dad was like most parents. I never heard of a parent sitting down with their child and, out of the blue, telling them all the gory details of their past life."

"But," people insist, "You would think your father would have told you he had been involved in the syndicate!" Well, he didn't. And so I learned about it that night watching The Wiretapper.

More details were filled in for me when I began to travel with my dad on Sunday mornings to hear him speak at chapel services for Pro Athletes Outreach. These services, organized for visiting professional football and baseball teams, were often held in the locker room in the bowels of Jack Murphy Stadium or at some hotel in San Diego. Being there with Dad gave me the chance to meet some of the biggest athletic stars of the day, the most memorable meeting being with Yogi Berra, who I met in the stadium locker room, with Berra wearing only his underwear, when he was manager for the New York Mets.

As the years went by, in similar ways, the many chapters of my dad's amazing life story were eventually revealed to me. And it was through my father that I first became familiar with a famous quote, which I have subsequently come to believe sums up his life, and really every life. Blaise Pascal, a 17th-century French philosopher and mathematician, wrote in his *Pensées*:

> *What else does this craving, and this helplessness, proclaim but that there was once in man a true happiness, of which all that now remains is the empty print and trace? This he tries in vain to fill with everything around him, seeking in things that are not there the help he cannot find in those that are, though none can help, since this infinite abyss can be filled only with an infinite and immutable object; in other words by God himself. God alone is man's true good . . .*

My father, like everyone else on planet earth, had such an abyss. For the first thirty years of his life, he tried to fill that emptiness with all sorts of things that didn't satisfy. Then he found the one "infinite and immutable object" which eventually filled his emptiness. Once he received the "true good" of the Spirit of God, my father spent the rest of his life sharing with others out of God's fullness. What follows is the story of how it all transpired.

PART ONE:

Filling the Emptiness

(1919-1949)

1

Born and Raised in Los Angeles

That's how Dad would invariably begin one of his talks, whether it was speaking to professional athletes or the Oilmen of America: "I was born and raised in the City of Los Angeles." We always told him he sounded like the beginning of the TV drama, *Dragnet*. But he wouldn't listen to us. The story was always told the same way, so I came to know it rather well. In fact, I came to know my father's life story so well that on one occasion when invited to tell the story at a dinner party, I was able to relate the "Reader's Digest Condensed Version" of my father's life history as though playing back a tape recorded message.

Boylston Street was where it all started for Dad. We drove by the ramshackle old house one afternoon in 1990 before my wife and I took my parents to see *The Phantom of the Opera* at the Dorothy Chandler Pavilion. Dad said the house had lost the charm and warmth of the early 1920's. Indeed it had, a dilapidated and forlorn looking building in the middle of the barrio, overlooking downtown Los Angeles and its skyscrapers, buildings that never existed when my father was born on February 17, 1919. My Aunt Betty, my father's elder sister by one year, remembers the telephone number was Broadway 1607. The address is the same today as it was then: 421 North Boylston. .

Dad's father, James Arthur Vaus, Sr., Grandpa Jim to me, was a Baptist preacher, a dean and professor of Hebrew and Old Testament at the Bible Institute of Los Angeles, known as Biola. He was a hard-working, studious man. He wore glasses, and his thick pompadour turned grey early in his life, perhaps from prolonged hours of study. His manner was always gracious and patient. He became such an expert in Hebrew, Old Testament Messianic prophecy and Rabbinical theology that even local rabbis would sometimes come to have him settle their theological disputes.

Grandpa Jim insisted that his children attend Sunday school and church every week. The Vaus children were not allowed to go to movies or dances. Grandpa Jim was thoroughly committed to his religious beliefs and readily presumed his children would share his faith. But to Dad, family worship at home was a bore. He participated as expected, but his heart wasn't in it.

Grandpa Jim and Grandma Lillie originally met at Biola as two of the first students at the school. My grandmother being Jewish and my grandfather being a Gentile made for an interesting combination. When they wanted to hide conversation from their children's listening ears they would talk in a combination of Yiddish and German. In later years, they founded together the Los Angeles Hebrew Mission, a Christian outreach to Jewish people, and they operated a small mission church in Echo Park. The Angelus Temple of Aimee Semple McPherson fame was right around the corner.

Grandpa Jim came from a long line of devout Christians. Grandpa Jim's father, Quincy Tilghman Vaus, a farmer from Illinois, lived with Grandpa Jim and Grandma Lillie in Los Angeles during the last years of his life. I still have a photo of Quincy's father, Tilghman Warren Vaus, holding a Bible. He lived his life as a farmer in Ohio, but was born in Maryland in 1806. The family traces its roots back to five brothers, sons of a wealthy and famous doctor in England, who came to the Virginia Colony in the 1640's.

James Vaulx (as the family name was spelled back then) was one of the first vestrymen of the Bruton Parish Church in Williamsburg. The family was of the landed gentry who originally came to England from France with William the Conqueror in 1066.

Grandma Lillie, on the other hand, was a Jew who had converted to the Christian faith in 1896 when she was but twelve years old, living with her family in Pittsburgh, Pennsylvania. For years she stood alone in her Christian faith, until her mother and sister eventually accepted Jesus as their Messiah. Grandma Lillie had a zeal for winning her fellow Jews to Jesus. She often said that there was nothing sadder to her than a Jew who did not know that his or her Messiah had already come. She was a charter student of Biola and later the founding director of the department of Jewish Evangelism at the same school.

Grandma Lillie was a dainty woman—fastidious, with an earnest, intense nature. I gather from comments Dad made years later that she was a rather dominant personality in the home. She could be argumentative, confrontational and outspoken. As a result, when he became a husband and father, Dad shied away from any confrontation or argument in the home. He would walk away rather than continue a heated discussion. He wanted the waters around him to be smooth as glass.

So it was into a zealous, if seldom placid, Christian family that my father was born at Angelus Hospital in early 1919. Dad's earliest memory was of a later hospital stay. The room was dark, the walls were green and the bed was high. From a door behind him the nurses in white came and went. Dad was later told how at almost sixteen months of age his great curiosity had led to catastrophe. He had turned a boiling pot of water from a stovetop on to his head. Dad was scalded from top to bottom. Doctors told Grandpa Jim and Grandma Lillie that he had little chance of survival.

My mother still has the original telegram, addressed to Grandma Lillie, from Chicago, Illinois, dated August 6, 1920, which

reads as follows: "Your message received and my loving sympathy goes out to you both in this affliction. Have requested the Great Commission Prayer League to unite with us in prayer for the little sufferer and send Acts 3:16."

The sender was Mrs. A. G. Wells. Her husband was the CEO of the Union Pacific Railroad. Acts 3:16 (NIV) says: "By faith in the name of Jesus, this man whom you see and know was made strong. It is Jesus' name and the faith that comes through him that has given this complete healing to him as you can all see." Dad recovered from the scalding with only one small scar on his side.

2

945

A few months after the scalding incident, my father's family moved from Boylston Street to East Edgeware Road, a horseshoe shaped street in an area known as Angelino Heights. In later years, Dad always referred to that house simply using the street number: 945. Shortly after their move to Edgeware Road, a sister, Virginia, was added to the family.

Beautiful in those early years, Edgeware Road was part of a desirable neighborhood, but a railroad track ran down the middle of the dirt road. Part of the Los Angeles Railroad system, the streetcar was very small. They called it "the dinky." It was the shortest line in the system, less than ten blocks. It ran from Temple Street up Edgeware Road, turned on Douglas and ended at Kensington.

The Vaus family home was middle class: a two-story wood frame building, set back off the street, behind a row of cedar trees, on one of the many hills of Los Angeles. There was plenty of lawn for my father to mow once he was old enough for that chore. The rugs inside were not thick and the drapes weren't brocade, so my father somehow concluded his parents were poor. There were plenty of other people who had less than the Vaus family during the Depression Era. But because my father couldn't have all the

things he wanted, he decided his parents must be poor and that their poverty was due to their Christianity.

In fact, they were not poor at all. The Vaus family even had a maid, an African American lady named Myrtle, who kept the house clean and prepared meals so that Grandma Lillie could focus on her work of Jewish evangelism and teaching Bible studies. And Grandpa Jim had a secretary by the name of Pearl Piatt.

During his first six years of schooling at Cortez Street School, Dad did poorly in English and math. But he greatly enjoyed ringing the bell to signal recess or lunch hour; he liked having to leave the classroom and go to the office to perform his task. The principal of the grammar school told Grandma Lillie that her son "would run the school if we let him. What's more—he could do it!"

Grammar schools in those days usually had at least one boy who stood out as a bully. The one at Dad's school made it difficult for every kid. Dad knew the time would come when he would have to face him down. He talked to his father about it, and Grandpa Jim gave him lessons in how to defend himself, how to "hold his dukes" as he put it. Not many days later, Dad had his chance. Challenged by the bully, he soon found himself swinging his arms in desperation. It seemed like the whole student body was rooting for him. The bout ended successfully for my father and from that day on, the bully gave him a wide berth.

In addition to being able to defend himself, Grandpa Jim wanted his son to learn to play the violin; perhaps he had dreams of him becoming the next Jascha Heifetz. In fact, Grandpa was so interested in that particular instrument that he made his own violins as a hobby. He would boil varnishes in the kitchen and Grandma would try to run him out. The smell filled the entire house. Grandpa carved the scroll on his violins and was very particular on all the measurements. In the garage he had all kinds of patterns and partially completed instruments. However, violin practice was an-

other big bore to my father. His parents hired a teacher who came to the house to give violin lessons. Dad played in the school orchestra during grammar school but he hated it. He thought it was very feminine to play the violin and he had no desire to be girlish. He nevertheless continued playing the violin into his young adult years, even taking his instrument on a mission trip to Canada at the age of nineteen, along with three fellow college students.

From a young age my father had a rebellious streak. On one occasion, his father asked him to sweep the sidewalk in front of their home. Feeling the task a bit larger than what he wanted to tackle, Dad ran away instead—all the way to his aunt's house in Eagle Rock! When Dad's aunt called his parents to let them know of his whereabouts, Grandpa Jim and Grandma Lillie's worry gave way to astonishment that their son knew his way from Los Angeles to Eagle Rock, a distance of twenty miles. Knowing his way around town was an ability my father would put to good use in later life.

Dad was also on the mischievous side. One of his earliest acts of mischief that turned dangerous had to do with the fire department. The local fire house was on the corner of Temple and Edgeware Road. In the earliest days, the fire truck was a horse drawn wagon. Later, to make way for the freeway, the firehouse was moved one block to Bellevue and Edgeware. Edgeware became the main route for the fire dispatch; the Vaus family could always hear the truck going out from the firehouse to put out small trash fires, which occasionally called for the firefighters' expertise. It was nothing too spectacular, but the neighborhood children loved to see the fire engines out on a run.

My father, in particular, wanted to see something more spectacular; he wanted to see the action up close and personal. The Vaus family had a chicken house fenced with wire and covered over with vines, most of which were dry and very flammable. One day, Dad ignited some of the leaves and then ran down the driveway and in the front door of the house seventy-five feet away to wait

for something to happen. He could hear the engines coming from blocks away. His one match ignition had turned into a blazing inferno, catching on fire not only the hen house, but the next door neighbor's garage as well, stirring much excitement on the otherwise quiet, peaceful street. Neither his parents nor the authorities figured at the time that Dad was the guilty party. He just looked too angelic. The fire department said it was spontaneous combustion but Dad's sisters both had that all-knowing look. My Aunt Betty and Aunt Ginny would have made good detectives!

3

The Devil Loves a Shining Mark

Grandma Lillie, early on, recognized her son's talents, as well as his propensity toward getting into trouble. She would often warn him saying, "The devil loves a shining mark." By that phrase Grandma Lillie meant: "Satan tries especially hard to tempt people with talent." Be that as it may, many of Dad's "devilish" activities in his early years were quite tame.

One of the routine family events in those days was the Thursday trip to market. His mother went to a grocery store on Hill Street, in what is now considered downtown L. A. They rode the city transit system, or L. A. Railroad, as it was called. The system had larger street cars which ran on Temple Street and they would ride from Edgeware to Broadway, Broadway and Hill being the two main roads through downtown Los Angeles. Grandma Lillie shopped at the Grand Central Market on Hill Street between Second and Third Streets. A tunnel ran under Third Street not far from Angels Flight, the incline railway built in 1901.[2]

Grandma Lillie always wanted her son to look his best while accompanying her to market or going on shopping tours of any kind. Dad's first suit was wool, and of course the pants made him itch. So one day he prepared for the trip downtown by wrapping towels from the kitchen around his legs. Everything went well until the

towels started to slip. Grandma Lillie was terribly embarrassed as towels started appearing from her son's pant legs.

It was always more fun for my dad going shopping with his father. Grandpa Jim had a favorite stand in the market where Chinese food was served; he always ordered Egg Foo Yung. Chinese food remained a life-long favorite of my father, especially Egg Foo Yung.

His father also took the children on other trips. Grandpa Jim loved to drive his Chevrolet, with open sides and glasine windshield, through Elysian Park, now the home of Dodger Stadium. Other drives which were real adventures took the Vaus family to what were, in those days, remote locations, such as Hermosa, Manhattan and Redondo Beaches. The trip home always involved Grandpa Jim pretending to hear gurgling sounds. He would ask his children if they heard it too. This was the first tip-off that he was going to stop at the ice cream parlor; the gurgling sounds were from the fountain where they made delicious strawberry sodas.

On one particular trip to Hermosa Beach, Grandpa Jim had parked the car and the family was walking to the ocean. It was the Fourth of July and unbeknownst to his family, Dad had his pockets full of caps, which could be fired in realistic fashion from a toy gun. Unfortunately the caps also tended to fire off when rubbed; on this occasion that is exactly what happened. Dad's pants became a pyrotechnic display with hundreds of caps firing off, one after another in his pockets. His pants caught fire and so Grandpa Jim pushed him over to roll in the sand. His parents sympathized with their son's hot seat, but they disciplined him nonetheless.

A boarder in Dad's childhood home "sparked" a life-long interest in electronics. His name was Atwood Chambers and he was an L. A. streetcar conductor. At the age of nine, my father was intrigued by Chambers' change maker. Atwood kept it in his closet. Dad liked the way it shelled out coins when he put pressure on the levers. In fact, my father liked taking the money out, but he

never put it back. His mother and Atwood cornered him one day and asked if he had been taking change from the change maker. Dad was embarrassed at being caught and as things turned out, it was one of those times when Grandpa Jim applied the "board of education" to the "seat of his son's knowledge." After that experience my father confined himself to a common interest shared with Chambers–radios.

Atwood Chambers was a quiet man who loved tinkering with his gadgets. He was always buying wires and various parts and putting them together to make fascinating inventions. He would work on a radio with the meticulous attention of a watchmaker. Dad observed and became a self-appointed apprentice to the man. He treasured every electronic part Chambers threw away. My father began drilling holes and stringing wires like garlands all over the house. That habit continued throughout his life. Once when revisiting our old family home in Tarrytown, I was asked by the new residents: "What were all those holes for in the basement wall?" I just smiled and chuckled.

Dad soon inherited the old hayloft above the family garage as his special abode. Grandma Lillie probably couldn't stand one more buzzer system decking the hallways of her home. In his workshop retreat Dad experimented and built his own radios just like Chambers. He went on to teach himself more about the wonderful world of electronics.

Radio was in its infancy in those days. It was a great thrill to listen to a station coming in all the way from Pittsburgh-KDKA. Dad built radio receivers, and then radio transmitters, which he used on the ham frequencies. He didn't have a license to operate a ham station but that didn't matter; he made up his own call letters. The biggest excitement was when he got a response to his first call; it came from another teenager, seventy-five miles away on Mt. Wilson. His radio receiver and transmitter worked! Dad's best friend, Jimmy Thornburg, observed the feat and was duly impressed.

Next Dad got involved in the construction of power amplifiers; he played music which could be heard blocks away. He didn't win too many admirers among the neighbors but he and his buddies thought it was great.

After trial and error he managed to build a sound system for church. The leaders of the congregation put my father in charge of the system and the remote controls for the radio station that broadcast the morning service. The Vaus family attended the Church of the Open Door, a nondenominational congregation on Hope Street in downtown Los Angeles. The church met in a large building with thirteen floors, doubling as dormitory and classroom space for Biola. Years later when my parents took me on a tour of their old Los Angeles haunts we used to laugh at the church sign. It read simply: Jesus Saves. But underneath the church billboard was the sign for Crocker Bank. So read together it said: Jesus Saves Crocker Bank. In those days Crocker Bank needed saving. (The bank was eventually purchased by Wells Fargo.)

4

Teenage Rampage

One of the titles of my father's later books was: *Teenage Rampage*. While Dad's early teen years could hardly be characterized as a rampage they were interesting nonetheless.

At Church of the Open Door my father attended Sunday school, worship services, and the youth group called Christian Endeavor. Dad was elected president of the junior high youth group and later, the high school chapter. That's where most of his friends were and that's why he stayed involved. The high school department of Christian Endeavor had a great deal of social activity. On Fridays, the group would always go on outings. Grandma Lillie was concerned that her son was more interested in the social aspect of church than he was in Christ's message, but at least he wanted to be involved.

Dad's Sunday school teacher was a Mr. Brown. The Browns had a daughter and two sons. My father was interested in the daughter, but she never paid him the time of day. The two brothers were older than Dad, but he enjoyed visiting their house in Santa Monica on the weekends. They had great times together. The two Brown boys were baseball fanatics. They spent their summers playing for the Visalia Ball Club in Northern California. One of the boys was a pitcher and the other played catcher or second base. One sum-

mer Dad hitch-hiked to Visalia and spent a good part of summer vacation with the Brown boys. They were looking for someone to install radios in cars at the garage where they worked. Dad enjoyed the work, and the people he stayed with that summer provided fabulous meals with heaping platters of golden corn on the cob.

It was in high school that my father's interest in girls began in earnest, around the same time he learned to drive–on an old Model T Ford. Dad's first female interest was Sarah Jane. He knew her through school and worked up enough courage to go to her house to ask for a date. After a thorough examination conducted by Sarah Jane's parents, the date was approved. But Dad must not have been too impressed, because later he never remembered where they went or what they did on that date.

It was during this time period that my father also carried out his first wiretapping job. He learned that his sister's boyfriend planned to visit one evening. So Dad planted a microphone behind the sofa and broadcast the conversation to all who wanted to listen in the back yard!

My father graduated from Belmont High School in 1937. To please his father, Dad filled out an application for entrance to Biola and became a student there in September of '37. The course work was comprehensive for any young man planning to enter the ministry—doctrine, missions, psychology, Christian ethics, and evangelism were some of the subjects covered. Dad knew the strict standards of Biola, having visited the school often prior to enrollment, but his unrestrained spirit was frequently out of sympathy with the faculty. Perhaps for that reason, Dad left Biola in the fall of 1938 and attended Los Angeles Junior College for a semester. After an apparently unsuccessful stint there, Grandpa Jim and Grandma Lillie thought it was time for their son to try a campus away from home. It was decided that he should accept a scholarship he had won during high school to attend Wheaton College in Wheaton, Illinois. Some of his Biola friends saw him off from the train sta-

tion as he departed to travel eastward in January 1939. One of the girls gave him a poem he would often quote in later years: "Child of my love, fear not the unknown morrow..."

Up until that train trip to Wheaton, my father had only been outside of California one other time. His eyes remained fixed out the window, watching the shifting scenery as the train crossed the country. Years later he could still recall the mountains growing big as the train roared toward them, fading as the train left them behind, speeding on over the flat lands of the Midwest. In future years he would make the trip many times, but it was never as heady as that first time on his own.

At Wheaton my father roomed with Carl F. H. Henry, later to become a well-known evangelical theologian, and Richard C. Halverson, later to become the Senior Pastor of Fourth Presbyterian Church in Bethesda, Maryland and Chaplain of the United States Senate. Forty-six years later, Dick Halverson's recommendation helped me to gain entrance to Princeton Theological Seminary. As a student at Princeton and a leader in the Theological Student Fellowship, I invited Dr. Halverson and Dr. Henry to address our student body on the same day. Introducing Dr. Henry I told how my father had roomed with him at Wheaton and then gone on to be involved in organized crime. At that moment, Dr. Henry piped up and said, "And I went on to be involved in disorganized theology!"

Dad's first and only semester at Wheaton was pleasant, but bland, with C average grades. He wasn't expelled from the school, but during the summer back home in California, he received a letter from his college counselor telling him he wasn't making the most of his potential and urging him to buckle down if he should choose to return in the autumn.

My father chose not to go back to Wheaton, instead returning to the Bible Institute. The year he went back to Biola earned him a reputation for being a prankster when he performed his second wiretap escapade. Dad was mad at a girl named Annie for some

wisecrack she had made about him; he was ready to even the score. Dad was a scrapper—a trait inherited no doubt from his mother. One of his oft-repeated sayings was: "For two cents and a button I'll fix his wagon."

He was ready to "fix this girl's wagon" for her. The afternoon following the wisecrack, my father talked the elevator operator into running him up to the girl's dormitory on the top floor. The operator kept watch while Dad planted a microphone behind a mirror in Annie's room. He buried a loudspeaker under her bed and ran the wires out the window. He was able to slip back down on the elevator, undetected. Then he attached the wires from the loudspeaker to his equipment and went to dinner. He excused himself early from the cafeteria and went to his own dorm room to wait for the action to begin.

A half-hour dragged by before Dad heard Annie and her girlfriend enter their dorm room, giggling. The evening's topic, which they explored in great detail, was which boys they liked and why. He recorded the girls' debate and when it was "lights out" time he flipped the switch, and in a booming voice said: "Good evening girls, this is Fu Man Chu!" Quickly switching back, Dad could hear their reaction: screams, silence, and then a voice wailing, "He's under the bed! He's under the bed!" Flipping the switch again, he let the girls know who was really on the other end of the line. They chatted back and forth wittily. Annie thought it was a terrific prank until my father told her he had recorded the girls' earlier conversation. At first Annie didn't believe it, until Dad played her a portion. Then she was not only embarrassed—she was furious. When word of the wiretap got out, neither Grandpa Jim, nor the dean of the women, were as amused as my father was.

5

Unorganized Crime

Dad's first serious romantic interest was in a girl named Frances, a Biola student. She was a couple of years ahead of him in school, but Dad was fascinated with her. He was invited by Frances' widowed mother to come and visit their home in Butten Falls, Oregon, the summer before Dad re-entered Biola. He was also invited to fill the pulpit of Frances' home church. That summer he and Frances roamed the woods and the beautiful Oregon countryside, taking picnic lunches with them and enjoying lengthy discussions.

Dad fell in love, or so he thought at the time. Grandpa Jim advised him against entering into an engagement, but he felt it was the thing to do. He bought Frances a very simple, plain ring; word soon got around that they were engaged. By the time of the engagement Frances had finished school, but Dad still had a long way to go. Once he was back at Biola they corresponded by mail.

That same year my father was in charge of fund-raising for the Biolan, the annual college yearbook. Usually advertisements were sold to cover the cost of publishing. But Dad came up with another scheme: a show for the public on Sunday afternoon at the Church of the Open Door. Dad advertised that they would be talking to missionaries in South America and Africa by the miracle of long distance telephone. Three thousand people came. As the crowd

circulated on the night of the event Dad calculated the income from the offering that would be taken.

He discovered, however, that the Biolan only netted a hundred dollars, with the largest part of the offering being used for other purposes. Dad was furious and in that fury, he lost his reason. He decided to take off for Florida with the yearbook funds. He bought a plane ticket to fly from Burbank to Miami with a couple stops in between. His sudden disappearance brought no end of problems for the school and for his family. The school feared foul play and contacted the police. Dad's parents counseled: "Wait. He'll turn up."

Dad spent several days in Miami and finally called his folks to tell them he was alright. "Dare I return?" he asked. Grandpa Jim answered, "Yes, son. Yes." and wired his son the money to return home.

The train ride home was depressing. All that Dad could think about was the embarrassment and humiliation of facing family, friends and the school administrators. Dad borrowed money from a family friend, signing a note, to replace the funds he had stolen.

However, Biola expelled him anyway and he was told to stay away from the building and the students. The elders at Church of the Open Door shut their door on my father telling him, "Don't come back." At the time my dad most needed friends, Christian fellowship and counsel, the Church turned her back on him. Even the engagement with Frances was broken off and Dad became a loner.

During his limited free time as a student, my father had worked as a wrapper, or box boy, at the Broadway Department Store in downtown Los Angeles. Expelled from school, he began to work for Broadway full time. His paycheck was increased, but a hefty chunk of his fifty-cent per hour pay was going to pay off the Biola note. He chafed under the limitations this placed upon him. He wanted to go places with his friends, the other wrappers and delivery boys; he wanted to show off and be able to pay for them. Dad was always

generous, first with other people's money, later with his own. When a fellow worker named Schwartz hit him up for a twenty-dollar loan, Dad was eager to help. But he didn't have the money.

So, once again, Dad came up with a devious scheme. He went home at noon one day. He asked to borrow his father's car, a Studebaker sedan, and without his father's knowledge also borrowed his dad's 32-calibre nickel-plated Harrison-Richards revolver. The gun was old, rusty, and didn't work, but that didn't matter for what my father had in mind.

He went back to work the afternoon shift at the Broadway. Then he drove out to Beverly Hills, and cruised down a deserted street until he saw an elderly man, walking alone. Dad parked the car, walked up behind the man and, holding the gun in his right pocket, tapped the man on the shoulder and said: "This is a stick-up. Hand me your wallet."

After a second of shock, the man handed over his wallet. Dad stuffed it in his pocket and headed back to the car. The elderly man called after him: "May I have my driver's license back?"

Dad said: "Sure." He pulled the wallet out and let the man have his license back. When my father got back in the car he looked in the wallet. Imagine his disappointment when he found only fourteen dollars! Low in spirit, he drove to the home of a girlfriend. But she wasn't there. So he drove home and after giving his father a lame excuse for being out late with the car, he went to bed.

In the morning, still feeling very low, he went to work and was promptly met by the police who arrested him for armed robbery. Apparently while passing the elderly man his license, Dad's Broadway employee identification card fell out of his own pocket. The elderly man had picked it up and hurried off to the police. This was to be the first of many times that my father would make the newspaper headlines. This time it read: CALLING CARD BANDIT ARRESTED.

Dad's parents met him at the police station, along with his mother's brother who had been part of the L. A. political scene. No doubt they were hoping to be able to find a way to get him off, but by the time they got there my father had already admitted his guilt to the police and returned the fourteen dollars. Dad was confined for several days in the Beverly Hills Police Station. Seeking to teach him a lesson, his parents did not post bail. Grandpa Jim said the effect of the arrest was disastrous upon his work as a minister. But in the end every effort was extended to try to secure probation. Friends wrote letters. A job was promised. Grandpa Jim pleaded with the judge. But the fact that my father had used a gun, albeit one that wouldn't fire, coupled with the information that he had previously stolen money at Biola, led to the judge's decision to send Dad to the County Jail for one year.

By a quirk of destiny, my father was incarcerated in the Los Angeles County Jail at the same time as Benjamin "Bugsy" Siegel, the boss of Mickey Cohen, for whom my father would later work. However, there were a few differences in their treatment as prisoners. Siegel wore silk shirts and pleated pants whereas Dad wore the required blue denim. Siegel had a comparatively luxurious cell; Dad had a four-by-eight shared with another inmate. Dad and the other men did a lot of pick and shovel work; Siegel often roamed outside his cell not doing much work at all. Bugsy enjoyed the best food possible; my father and the rest of the prisoners suffered through pasty oatmeal, potato-laden stews and beans.

My father tried to make the best of his time in jail, even forming a choir and teaching the other men some of his favorite hymns. He bragged about his father, the preacher, and all the grand things he was going to do upon his release. After a couple of months in the County Jail, my father was transferred to the County Road Camp. The food was better, and he worked building a road to Malibu Lake. After several months, he was released on probation and took

a job in the Building and Grounds department of the University of California at Los Angeles. In his spare time he took classes at U. C. L. A. in science and math. Dad got involved again in church life, this time at Hollywood Presbyterian, where he became very active in the youth programs. But normal life was once again interrupted, this time by the Japanese attack on Pearl Harbor.

6

In the Army Now

Considering his criminal record, my father had no expectation that the army would accept him, but less than thirty days after Pearl Harbor, he received his draft notice. As he waved good-bye to his parents, he walked down Edgeware Road to Douglas Street. Two of the corner lots were vacant. One was the neighborhood play lot, used for "Kick the Can", baseball and other fun and games. As he headed down Douglas, Dad could still see his folks waving, until he passed the empty lot. From there it was mostly down hill to Sunset Boulevard. Three more long blocks and he was at the community draft office.

He joined a half dozen other young men, eagerly awaiting their new life in the army. The civilian in charge gave them instructions for transportation via the red streetcar to San Pedro. From there the army would transport them to Fort McArthur. Dad was put in charge of the large brown envelope containing all the information on each inductee. Midway through the hour-long ride, he managed a look inside. He saw a brief description of his bout with the law. Nothing else was on that piece of paper, so he tore it up.

A few days later, Dad was sent with about thirty others to Camp Callan, situated on a piece of land which would later belong to the University of California at San Diego, my alma mater. Life at

Camp Callan consisted of a combination of boot camp indoctrination and basic training. The men soon had their uniforms and in no time at all, Dad had that feeling: You're in the army now! For the thirty days that followed, it was drill, rifle range and study.

The army wasted no time in putting the new draftees on duty. After Pearl Harbor, everyone was jittery and expecting invasion by small craft along the California coast. Dad's guard duty was three or four hours in length, during the wee hours of the morning.

After taking an aptitude test, my father was asked to consider attending Officer Candidate School. He accepted the opportunity and was sent to Wilmington, North Carolina. Dad graduated first in his class, was made a second lieutenant, and was soon appointed regimental course instructor in mathematics, which included algebra, logarithms, trigonometry and coordinates.

By the fall of 1942, he was assigned to the 37th Antiaircraft Brigade under the Fourth Army in California. While there, my father experienced a quick succession of promotions. December 2, 1942, he was appointed Cryptographic Security Officer. December 24, he was promoted to first lieutenant. January 1943, Dad was appointed as member of the board for examining applicants for promotion to warrant officer. In July of '43, he was appointed by General Hardaway to serve as member of the court martial board.

As a field and range officer, my father served at Victory and Magnolia Boulevards, in North Hollywood, near the Lockheed Aircraft plant. Four guns were stationed there, heavily camouflaged. Looking back it seems a mild assignment, but at the time, enemy attacks were expected. Los Angeles had several air-raid warnings during the war, and Lockheed seemed a logical spot for the enemy to strike.

Radar was brand new and Dad's unit was one of the first to be issued radar equipment. It wasn't too well understood. Processing information obtained by radar was slow. It took three men to correctly aim and fire a gun. So while my father was off-duty he

experimented for hours at a time trying to figure out a mechanism that would both calculate and aim the gun.

A captain walked past one day and told my father he was "molesting government property." At that moment the commanding general of the 37th Brigade also walked by. He stopped to investigate and listen to the captain's complaint. A few days later, Dad was called into the general's office and questioned. He explained what he was trying to do and consequently the instrument he designed was accepted for use by the army. He was assigned a job that, on the Table of Organization, called for a lieutenant colonel. My father was made Signal Officer in Charge of Tactical Communication and Radar Defensive Network.

Dad spent three years at that station and obtained the rank of captain. However, my father still had a bad habit of "being generous" with other people's property. Within his reach were government priorities, the authority to allocate goods belonging to the army. It became common knowledge that a man could always get a priority for photographic equipment from Vaus. For some of the priorities, Dad picked up a few extra dollars to spend on his leave time in Hollywood.

7

Hollywood Presbyterian Church

One of the entities to which Dad loaned army equipment at that time was the First Presbyterian Church of Hollywood , though I am sure the church was unaware of how my father obtained the equipment. Called "Hollywood Pres" by many, it was the largest church in its denomination at the time, led by Louis Evans, Sr. and Assistant Pastor Richard Halverson. Dad got involved in the college and career department, led by Henrietta Mears, which was filled with a variety of people—movie stars as well as future church leaders: Bill Bright (later founder of Campus Crusade for Christ), Connie Haynes (a singer with Bob Hope), Rhonda Fleming and Colleen Townsend (both movie actresses), and Louis Evans, Jr. (the pastor's son). Dad became best friends with Don Swann, Johnny Johnson and Joel Allen, the movie actor. Together they built dreams for the future they hoped for once they were out of the armed forces.

For a while, my father dated Miss Mears' niece. Miss Mears was impressed enough that she wanted to send Dad to Princeton Theological Seminary after his military service was completed. However, that relationship didn't last. Dad developed interests in another quarter. He dated and ended up engaged to Lauralil Evans, the pastor's daughter.

Dad was involved in the leadership of two worship services on Sundays at Hollywood Pres. One was an afternoon service. Men from the church would gather soldiers off the streets of Hollywood and bring them into the sanctuary. Dad would lead the singing, deliver a message, and even give an evangelistic invitation.

The other service Dad was a part of was the Sunday evening worship service. He would invariably lead the singing, along with others. And it was at Hollywood Pres that one of the most important events in my father's life took place. It was there at the age of twenty-five that my father met a beautiful sixteen year old girl named Alice Rosealba Park.

It was in 1944 that my mother and her brother Bill, along with neighbor Virginia Mills, started attending the youth group at Hollywood Presbyterian Church. Mom later joined the college group even though she was too young. She has fond memories from that time period of trips to Forest Home Christian Conference Center, a camp pioneered by Henrietta Mears.

Mom first saw my father at Hollywood Pres, leading singing for the Sunday night service. My mother attended the service with her dad. When she first saw my father she turned to her dad and said: "That's the man I'm going to marry."

Even though Mom was bold in her aspirations, she was still too shy to approach Jim Vaus, in his captain's uniform. She pressed her friend Virginia into making introductions on the steps of Hollywood Pres, even though Virginia didn't know him!

Every Sunday night after the evening service there was a hymn-sing at someone's home. Sometimes the sing would be at the home of Henrietta Mears, sometimes at the home of Dr. Evans. After Mom was introduced to Dad, she and a car load of other girls would catch a ride with him to the hymn-sing.

My mother distinguished herself on one of these occasions. They were heading to Miss Mears' large home in Westwood. Dad was speeding in a government car. During those years my father

became quite recognizable for cruising Sunset Boulevard in a convertible with the army mascot, a lion cub, hanging out of the back. On this occasion Dad had six women in tow and Mom was in the backseat. They were pulled over by the Beverly Hills police for speeding. Dad jumped out of the car so quickly to greet the officer that he ripped his own pants down the back from top to crotch. Mom loaned her jacket so he could tie it around his waist until they got to Miss Mears' home where one of the ladies sewed his pants up for him.

One Sunday evening at a hymn-sing at Dr. Evans' house, my father announced his engagement to Lauralil Evans. My mother was devastated. All her hopes and dreams were dashed. She continued to have a sinking feeling every Sunday when she would look down from the balcony in the sanctuary at Hollywood Pres and see my father sitting next to Lauralil in the Evans' family pew. But unbeknownst to my mother, or my father, or the Evans family at that time, the engagement was not to last for very long.

8

Court-Martial

My father's ascent as an officer stopped at the rank of captain. The commanding general's request to promote him to major sent shock waves of dissension among the men passed over. Consequently, the promotion never materialized.

As already mentioned, Dad had acquired the reputation of being a soft touch for guys who wanted to buy automobiles, refrigerators and other items at military prices. My father would sign the priority forms even though he wasn't authorized to do so. A disgruntled officer who was disturbed by my father's speedy promotions turned him in. During the ensuing investigation, officers discovered an army projector Dad had appropriated for use at Hollywood Presbyterian Church. The fact that Dad fully intended to return the equipment didn't make any difference. He was charged with misuse of government priorities and misappropriation of government property, in short–theft.

In the fall of 1944, while my father was awaiting trial, he was allowed leave and suddenly showed up one Sunday night at a church hymn-sing. By this time, due to his mishaps in the army, Dad's engagement with Lauralil Evans was, understandably, broken off. My mother was in attendance at the hymn-sing along with another young man who had brought her. After the sing Dad asked if he

could give Mom a ride home. She quickly told the young man she had come with that she had other means of transportation.

Dad took her home. This time she was in the front seat, and her friend Virginia was in the back seat with Joel Allen. Dad dropped Joel and Virginia off first, then Mom. Once they were alone, Dad explained that the engagement with Lauralil was off. Mom and Dad held hands and had their first kiss. Dad warned Mom she might not hear anything from him for awhile, though he said nothing of his pending trial.

Mom didn't hear from Dad again until she received a Valentine card in February of 1945. That Valentine began a correspondence that lasted a year and a half. Dad had his buddies send letters and cards to my mother from various army locations during his subsequent imprisonment so that she would not be alerted to his status.

My father was sent to March Air Force Base in January 1945 where he was tried by court martial. Dad figured he would be kicked out of the army, but he wasn't prepared for what happened next. The officers in charge were ticked off because my father was remanded to their jurisdiction. Feeling that they were cleaning up someone else's mess, they hit him with the maximum sentence—ten years at hard labor—along with a dishonorable discharge from the army.

Anyone severed from the army, especially by court martial, was entitled to a review. My father was transferred to McChord Field in Washington State. Because he was still an officer he was allowed a certain amount of freedom on base while he awaited his review. Everyone he met tried to cheer him up. They all thought his case was too trivial for him to be sent to prison. Everyone expected a pardon. The Ninth Corps of the army did cut his sentence to five years, but he was sent to McNeil Island Federal Penitentiary.

While in prison Dad worked as an electrician, and taught school mathematics and elementary radio. Just as he had done in the L. A. County Jail, he joined the choir at McNeil Island—anything to make the time pass more quickly. While in the pen the announce-

ment came that Japan had surrendered. World War II was over. It was a wild, exciting night for all the prisoners, but the next day they settled back into routine.

Six months crept by while my father waited for presidential review. The justice system was slowed down following President Roosevelt's death. But in the end my father received a pardon from President Truman. He was ordered to Fort Leavenworth, Kansas for rehabilitation.

At that time General "Hap" Arnold decided that the army should share with colleges in the United States some of the radar information they had acquired during the war. Dad had a lot of that knowledge so he was assigned to the Air Force, and with a group of officers he toured the country, lecturing in colleges and universities.

In the midst of his travels with the Air Force, Dad was given enough time off to go on his first official date with Mom. The day was August 15, 1946. They went to Romeo's Italian Restaurant on Melrose in Hollywood. Dad knew the owner, and he was greeted by him as "Cap-e-tan!" Dad didn't bother to tell him, or my mother, about his court martial or his subsequent incarceration. That night Dad gave Mom his ID bracelet which read: "Captain James Vaus."

At the end of his lecture tour, in December 1946, Dad was finally given an honorable discharge from the army. He moved back in with his parents at 945 Edgeware Road and opened an electronic consulting service in Hollywood known as American Microlec.

9

The Wiretapper

The list of Dad's clients for his electronic engineering business eventually read like Who's Who in America. He designed and installed elaborate electronic equipment for large homes. For example, one of his clients was the well-known billionaire, J. Paul Getty.

In Getty's Malibu residence, Dad installed a custom-built radio system with outlets in twenty rooms and an intercom throughout the house. The gates and garage doors were wired so they would open electronically. Around the thirteen acre estate was a ring of infrared light for trespass control, another ring immediately around the house, and a third ring of infrared around Getty's bedroom. Getty feared something, perhaps kidnappers, and so he wanted his home to be as secure as it could be. Getty's fear turned out to be well founded in that his grandson was kidnapped years later.

All of the devices Dad used on Getty's home are commonplace today, but they were not so common in the 1940's. The most fun Dad had on that job was asking Getty to test the garage door opener. He got a kick out of ordering the richest man in the world in and out of the garage in his Cadillac.

In the midst of this heady time, my father's official wiretapping career began with him managing a high-class apartment building in Hollywood. Dad had volunteered to manage the apartments for

a friend, for a short period of time. During my father's tenure as manager, the tenants started insisting that he do something about one of their fellow tenants, a girl named Marge. She was a brunette who dressed with class. Marge kept to herself as far as the other tenants were concerned, but the problem was she had too many assorted male friends dropping by her apartment. Apparently she entertained these men in her apartment for money.

Dad phoned the Los Angeles Police Department and they sent three young detectives, Stoker, Dawson and Riley, from the vice squad to check things out. Dad explained the situation and Stoker asked, "Is anyone visiting Marge right now?"

"Yes, I think so. That is, she was walking down the hall with a stranger a couple of minutes ago."

Dad told the officers the apartment number and they went up to scope out the situation. As they approached the door they heard voices from inside. However, the sound was too muffled to understand what the people were saying. Dad suggested they try listening from the outside window. But that was no better. My father asked, "Don't you have a device that will allow you to listen behind closed doors?" The officers looked at him as if he was from another planet. "No, we sure don't." So my father offered to set up such a system for the police to listen in on Marge's activities.

Within twenty-four hours Dad had hidden a microphone in a vase in Marge's apartment while she was out at the grocery store. The microphone was connected to a wire recorder. The next night the police returned to listen in on Marge and her male friend for the evening. The end result: Marge was arrested for violating City Ordinance MC 4107.

The police department was so impressed with my father's wire-tapping abilities that they showed up a week later with more work for him to do. One of his biggest jobs for the police was busting the Hollywood madam, Brenda Allen. Newspapers described her as the "Hollywood Vice Queen." The problem in catching her was that this

smart madam didn't run a house, she ran her call girls strictly by phone, working through a switchboard. Brenda's name was listed in The Players Directory, a catalog of actors, and she bribed taxi drivers to hand out her business cards. Brenda developed a clientele that included many of the famous faces of the 1940's.

The officer in charge of the vice squad, Lieutenant Blair, was a tough cop who wanted Brenda Allen out of business. Brenda was spreading the word around that she had the vice on her payroll. Blair said it wasn't true and he was angry about it. Dad asked what was stopping Blair from nailing Brenda Allen.

"She's not stupid, that's the problem. She runs her business by phone. She sends her girls to meet men at different places, never the same, and never at her home. We don't even have Allen's phone number or any idea where she lives."

What the lieutenant needed was a device that would allow the vice squad to listen in on Allen's telephone conversations without anyone ever knowing they were doing so. Blair also wanted to know the phone number that was dialed. There would be other uses for this type of equipment as well–like breaking up bookmaking rackets.

It took my father a few weeks, in his off time, to develop an impulse indicator to determine the phone number dialed as well as making a device to bug a conversation without contacting the line. Just as he finished designing the equipment, the police also had a break in the case; they got hold of Brenda's address. My father tapped her phone line so the police could hear her scheduling appointments. They traced the number dialed and then tailed her to her appointment. The police dogged Brenda's every step until they caught her red-handed and she was convicted for pandering.

The case was reported in banner headlines in the newspaper. Some of the headlines were about my father and his wire recordings. Police officials were keen to get hold of those recordings, so much so that they staked out my father's place of residence at that

time and dug up the back yard looking for the recordings. Dad told the police he didn't have what they were looking for. So they had my father jailed for twenty-four hours before he was finally able to convince them he really had destroyed the tapes. That was the only time during my father's criminal career that he was beaten up—and that was by the LAPD!

10

Honeymoon on the Side

In the midst of all these nefarious activities, my father began dating my mother regularly, but at first he continued playing the field. He even managed to take my mother and another woman, Barbara, on the same date. Apparently he had double-booked! Why the two women consented to go out with my father, together, on the same night, I have never been able to figure out. My mom called Barbara to ask her what she was going to wear for the evening. Barbara said, "Casual." so that's how my mother dressed, only to find Barbara decked out in pearls and a black dress when they picked her up that night. The three of them went to a movie in Westwood and I guess my mother won the contest because she was taken home last.

Mom got to know Dad's family and even became good friends with his sister Virginia. One night early in 1947, Virginia invited Mom to go out dancing at the Palladium. She urged my mother not to put up with any more of my father's shenanigans. Afterwards they went home to 945 Edgeware Road, and my mother spent the night. Imagine my father's surprise when he came downstairs to breakfast the next morning and saw my mother seated with his family at the dining room table!

Dad took Mom to work that day and en route she gave him her ultimatum–either marriage, or their relationship would be off. Dad

called Mom that night and proposed. After the phone call he went over to my mother's home and asked her father for her hand in marriage. The Parks weren't thrilled at first with my father as a suitor for their daughter. My grandmother, Nana, was convinced my father was up to no good. But they consented to the marriage anyway.

My father didn't give my mother an engagement ring; he had already been engaged twice and never received the rings back when the engagements were broken, so I guess he wasn't taking any chances. To later make up for this slight my father gave my mother a very large diamond ring on their twenty-fifth wedding anniversary.

My parents were married on my mother's nineteenth birthday, in 1947. My mother's sister Helen was the maid of honor. Mom pressed Helen's dress that day and burned a place on it. (Perhaps that is why years later, when Mom taught me how to iron clothes, she warned me about not leaving the iron on the fabric for very long!) My parents were married at Aunt Betty and Uncle Lester's church, Christ Community Church in Canoga Park. Grandpa Jim and Uncle Lester performed the ceremony.

While driving away from the wedding reception, Mom scratched Dad's eyeball while waving out of the back of the limousine. That first night they went home to their newly rented, furnished, two-bedroom house, situated on a half acre on Strom Avenue in North Hollywood. The next day Dad went to the eye doctor, and the following day they left in a Ford convertible on their honeymoon.

The honeymoon consisted of a drive across the United States during which my father tried to peddle his impulse indicator. It was really a business trip with a honeymoon on the side. One stop was in Pittsburgh. Dad journeyed into the old stone police headquarters in downtown Pittsburgh and asked for an audience with the superintendent.

"Nobody gets to see him without an appointment," barked the sergeant.

"How about the assistant superintendent?" Dad queried.

"You'll have to wait."

Dad did wait, two or three hours, before the sergeant called his name and pointed the way to the assistant superintendent's cubical. Dad demonstrated the impulse indicator for the assistant. He was so fascinated he called the superintendent in. They had never seen anything like it, so they bought one. At the conclusion of the visit the superintendent invited Mom and Dad out for dinner. He arranged for a tour of the city prior to the evening meal, and their chauffeur was none other than the desk sergeant, who suddenly became the most polite gentleman in the world!

Dad tried the same routine in New York but the New York City Police could not be bothered. From there it was on to my parent's main destination: Washington DC. The FBI was very interested in the indicator and asked if they could hold on to the device for a brief period of time. Dad left one with them. Months went by and the FBI neither replied nor returned the device. Dad finally called the FBI on the phone, only to be told they weren't interested. He asked for his impulse indicator back. It was delivered by an unidentified messenger. Dad later learned that the FBI had duplicated his device. That incident ended my father's interest in marketing and selling his inventions.

11

Private Detective

My father didn't make much money working for the police. So, to ease his cash flow problem, he ordered electronic equipment using forged purchase orders. He usually chose major movie studios to sponge off of. He would have the equipment delivered to a phony address, then pick it up, but have it charged to the studio. Dad saved a lot of money that way and the police never knew they were solving crimes with stolen equipment.

Wiretapping for the LAPD, along with all the publicity from the Brenda Allen case, led to my father working for a man named Barney Ruditsky, a retired New York cop who ran a private detective agency on the Sunset Strip. Not long after my parent's return from their honeymoon, Barney called up Dad to say, "Hey Jim, I've got a hot job for you if you can get over here right away." My father responded pronto. When he arrived in Barney's office he found the actor, Mickey Rooney, sitting there along with his manager and attorney. The manager was holding a fan made up of five one-hundred-dollar bills. Rooney said, "It's for you, Vaus, if you can tap into the phone number on this piece of paper in the next five minutes."

My father was a big man, 250 pounds at the time, but he could move fast when he wanted to. Before the five minutes were up he was recording a conversation on the desired phone number.

"That's my houseboy," laughed Rooney. "He's making a bet. And he always loses money on the ponies, poor guy!"

Rooney wasn't in Barney Ruditsky's office to listen to his houseboy. But five minutes later he got what he wanted. My father recorded a conversation where Rooney's wife was talking intimately to another man. This got Rooney and his lawyer the evidence they needed for Rooney's upcoming divorce case and my father received $500 for fifteen minutes of work.

At that time in the State of California, there were a number of legal grounds for divorce, but property had to be divided equally unless one spouse could prove that the other had committed adultery. That day in Barney Ruditsky's office, my father hit the vein of a gold mine. Rooney referred Dad to another actor, whose wife was having an affair with someone else in the entertainment industry. And this was only the beginning. Hollywood was playing a game of musical beds that would make any television soap opera look tame by comparison. Consequently, my father made a lot of cash off of these movie stars and other notables.

There were no collection problems in this line of work either. If someone wouldn't pay my father for the work he had done, he would threaten to sell the recording to the spouse. This was usually enough to get payment in full, immediately. If it wasn't, then Dad would sell to the other side of the family.

There were moments when my father nearly got caught, like the time he set out to bug actress Joanne Dru's house. Dad was flat on his back in the crawl space under the house when he heard footsteps above. He stayed hidden until there was no more noise for quite some time then he casually crawled out from underneath the house. Unfortunately one of Joanne Dru's neighbors was watching, but that didn't fluster Dad. He just picked up his toolbox, waved and then took off in his car. He found in these sorts of situations that if he acted confident, no one paused to ask questions.

Soon Dad's wiretapping business grew. It came to include private companies spying on their competitors as well as politicians investigating their rivals. But that was nothing compared to the door of opportunity that was about to open for him.

12

Mickey Cohen

I well remember the time our family watched the movie Bugsy, starring Warren Beatty, in the movie theater. It was a rather gruesome but accurate portrayal of Bugsy Siegel's rise to one of the top spots in syndicated crime. The movie ended with Siegel's brutal murder by machine gun fire in actress Virginia Hill's home. After the movie I had only one question for my father: "Did Mickey Cohen really talk like that? Did he use so much profanity?" My father answered with a simple "Yes." Only Cohen never talked like that in front of me. He was the perfect gentleman whenever women and children were present.

Meyer Harris "Mickey" Cohen was a New York Jew who grew up as a prizefighter and then became a manager within the world of boxing. Indeed, he fought his way to the top of west coast gangland. As *Life* magazine once put it, Cohen was a "flamboyant five-five fireplug who learned the Celebrity Gangster style from the master, Bugsy Siegel. Cohen was one of Siegel's guys when Bugsy got bopped in 1947, and he inherited his mentor's Los Angeles bookmaking enterprises."[3] But even that inheritance did not come without a fight. Mickey soon found himself in turf wars with Jack Dragna, another syndicate boss; it was a war known as the Battle of Sunset Strip.

The first time my father met Mickey Cohen, he had but a hazy notion of who the man was. Dad only knew what the newspaper headlines said about Cohen. He was dubbed "The Czar of Sunset Strip" and "Hollywood's Gambling Haberdasher." One of Cohen's henchmen came to fetch my father at his place of business, American Microlec. The meeting took place at Cohen's haberdashery on Sunset Boulevard. Today it would be the type of shop one would find only on Rodeo Drive–clothes stored in vaults behind sliding doors matching the polished walnut walls, the salesman dressed to the nines. Dad explained to the salesman why he was there and the message was relayed to the back office.

My father had to wait while Cohen was being fitted for a suit. When he was summoned, Dad walked past the steel-plated door into Cohen's inner sanctum. It became quite clear that no one saw Mickey without an invitation. Cohen, even more immaculately dressed than the salesman, sat behind a circular desk with a portrait of FDR on the wall behind him. No one spoke. To fill the silence my father offered his name: "I'm Jim Vaus."

Without missing a beat Cohen shot back: "Vaus, I've been told the police planted a microphone in my house. Did you do it?"

Amazed, my father responded, "No, Mr. Cohen, I don't even know where you live."

Still sizing up my father with his brown eyes, Cohen pursued: "If there was a bug in my house could you find it and take it out."

Truthfully Dad answered back, "Mr. Cohen, I'm in the business of putting them in; I don't take them out."

At this, Cohen reached into his pocket and pulled out a wad of hundred dollar bills and started peeling them off one by one. "Vaus, what business did you say you were in?" he inquired.

"I think it's about to expand," was the reply.

My father was led by one of Cohen's lieutenants, Neddie Herbert, to his home in Brentwood. As though they were tip-toeing through the tulips, Neddie led Dad on a tour of the house, making

not a sound as they went. Dad was most impressed with Mickey's wall-to-wall closet filled with suits. And he was forced to wait while Cohen was fitted for another one! After the house, Dad and Neddie took a tour of the back yard. Dad did some digging and unearthed a rubber-covered lead cable that had been planted in the ground with surgical precision.

To locate the listening device, Dad unplugged all the electrical appliances in the house. His electric meter still registered a current. He then unscrewed every fuse in the fuse box until he located the right one. Then he used a device he had made to track the flow of the current. He traced it to the fireplace. Rather than rip up the floor Dad cut a hole in the wood storage box. Then he had to get his six-foot-four inch, 250-pound frame through that hole. Neddie was probably betting he couldn't do it. But there were hundreds of dollars at stake, so my father managed to squeeze through that tight spot.

Once under the house he turned his flashlight on and presto, there was the amplifier, only a few feet away. Dad relayed the message to Neddie who told him to sit tight until Cohen showed up. My father waited for an hour and a half for Mickey to get there and see for himself. Then it took about fifteen minutes for Dad to dislodge himself from the coffin-like space.

Afterwards, my father met with Cohen, who offered him several more hundred-dollar bills as a bonus. Then Cohen asked Dad to do another job for him—setting up electronic devices to protect him. Mickey was the only person in my father's business life at that time who never asked him to do a wiretap.

The next day my father realized the extended reach of Cohen's power. Somehow Mickey obtained a complete log of the conversations the police had recorded at his home; it was clear that Cohen had all the connections he needed to get done whatever he wanted.

Cohen's business, for which the haberdashery was only a front, was bookmaking. Unlike today, in the late 1940's, off-track betting

was illegal. Perhaps Cohen was just ahead of his time. As to formal education, Cohen had only progressed as far as graduating from grammar school, but he was a genius at keeping bets, wins, losses, and all the best horses sorted out in his brain. Mickey didn't want any written evidence that could be used against him in court. The LAPD kept a constant eye on Cohen's activities. They would have liked nothing better than to bust up his bookmaking racket. But they couldn't. Cohen was too sharp to let that happen. Plus, all of Cohen's buddies were too loyal.

When the Los Angeles County Grand Jury started investigating the L. A. syndicate, all of Mickey's power was turned against the police. My father was one of those who falsely testified against an innocent police sergeant, E. V. Jackson. The evidence was twisted to make it appear that Jackson was in league with Brenda Allen. Jackson ended up being evicted from the LAPD and the investigation of Mickey Cohen stopped.

13

Life and Death

For a while my father worked both for Cohen and the police department. Mickey didn't seem to mind for some reason. But after some time it became too difficult for my father to burn the candle at both ends. He had to make a choice. Cohen paid more, and it was all in cash–no need to report to the IRS. My father's decision was made for him.

Dad's main job during this time was to protect Cohen during the Battle of Sunset Strip. In order to be closer to the action, he moved his electronics business into the basement of Cohen's haberdashery. During this time, Cohen had to keep a low profile in order to prevent his head being shot off. He was under constant threat. The most dangerous time was when he would travel from home to office and back again. Dad designed an electronic signal board for Cohen's office by which Mickey could notify his escorts of his route home. He rigged a switch in Mickey's car by which he could turn the lights on throughout his property when he returned home after dark. Dad arranged a ring of infrared light around Cohen's home, similar to the one he had used on the Getty estate. And finally, he electrified the garage so that Cohen could open the door, drive right in, and close it immediately.

One dark evening, Cohen was driving home and switched on the lights on his estate. He opened the garage door like usual and headed up the driveway. As he did so, the car was barraged with gunfire from both sides. The windshield shattered. Mickey dropped to the floor and gunned the engine into reverse. He drove blind to Wilshire Boulevard and then reappeared at the wheel. The second time he went home that night he fortified himself and Neddie Herbert with plenty of firepower, but the snipers had taken off.

Another evening as Cohen drove down Sunset Boulevard he was hailed by friend, Frank Sinatra. But Mickey didn't respond. He smelled trouble and he didn't want Sinatra getting in the middle of it. Mickey's sixth sense was on target. Up the road a piece his car was again pelted with machine gun fire.

My father skirted death on a couple of occasions as well. Relaxing at Cohen's house one night the alarm rang out, indicating the infrared barrier had been trespassed. Dad sprang out of his easy chair and ran outside. His peripheral vision picked up a flicker of light sprinting across the lawn–a lighted fuse. Dad grabbed the fuse and a six-inch bomb rolled out of a hiding place underneath the house. My father quickly dislocated the fuse and just stood there for a moment, contemplating how close they had all come to death.

My dad saw men killed right in front of him. Hooky Rothman, another one of Cohen's soldiers, was shot one day on the way into my father's office at Mickey's place. One of Mickey's compulsions saved his own skin that day.

Cohen had a clean fetish. Perhaps he was a bit like Lady Macbeth trying to rub other men's blood off his hands. But it wasn't just Cohen's hands that had to be clean. His morning bath took hours. Brushing his teeth alone required thirty minutes and a whole tube of toothpaste. He never wore a suit more than a couple of times; that's why he had hundreds of them, each no less than $300 a piece. He only wore shoes as long as they looked like they

were fresh out of the box and the same with hats. Years later when I met Cohen he wouldn't pick up the phone without taking a few tissues with which to hold the receiver.

On the day Hooky was shot and killed, Cohen was on his way into my father's office. As was his custom, Mickey didn't bother to greet anyone on his way in; he headed straight for the men's room to wash his hands. Gunmen were dogging Cohen's heels, but when they fired, Cohen had disappeared into the men's room and Hooky caught the bullet meant for Mickey, right in the face. The incident jarred my father's psyche enough to make him think, if only momentarily, about life and death and God.

The next guy to get bumped off was Neddie Herbert. Once again he got the bullet intended for Cohen, except this time the shoot-out was at Sherry's Restaurant on the Sunset Strip. After a few of these incidents, Cohen picked up the practice of moving around with an entourage of bodyguards. The newspapers dubbed the group: Snow White and the Seven Dwarfs.

However, Mickey Cohen's life wasn't always filled with bombs and gunfire. There were quieter, happier times my father was privileged to share. There were always ten or twelve people invited for dinner at Cohen's house, even when he wasn't at home. Mickey always made sure a supply of sexy starlets was on hand for his guests. According to my father, Cohen wasn't interested himself; he was devoted to LaVonne, his wife of eighteen years. But Mickey wanted to be the proper host to famous celebrities like George Raft and Red Skelton, as well as noted businessmen and lawyers.

Entertaining away from home was very expensive for Cohen. Where his clean fetish helped him out on other occasions, it got him into trouble at nightclubs. In those days Mickey wouldn't keep any cash in his pocket that wasn't new and clean. His bookkeeper made sure he never ran short of pocket money; he supplied Mickey with anywhere from $800 to $1500 cash every day, so that Mickey's pockets wouldn't get dirty. Cohen became a target for waiters

and waitresses. When the restaurant would give him his change, the staff made sure it was doled out in old, grimy bills. Cohen wouldn't touch it, so the wait staff would end up with their biggest tips that way.

At this time, Dad's life was not totally consumed by the syndicate. He did have a home life. Mom and Dad lived in their rented house in North Hollywood until the spring of 1948, when they bought a two-bedroom house in the middle of a walnut grove on Main Street in Baldwin Park. Dad even did the wallpapering and painting for Mom. In those days it was a forty-minute drive from home to office.

After the broken engagement with Lauralil Evans at First Presbyterian Church of Hollywood, that no longer seemed like the best place to attend worship service. So my parents went to church at South Hollywood Presbyterian. They joined the church as members and even got involved in youth ministry there, hosting parties for the youth at their Baldwin Park home.

My parents had only been married for about three months when Mom got pregnant. So one day in November 1948, Mom called Dad at the office to tell him her labor was beginning. Within the hour he arrived with the ambulance, and contrary to the later portrayal in the movie *Wiretapper*, Dad was there for the birth of his first child, just as he was present for the births of each of his children. My sister Madeline was born at Queen of Angels Hospital. As Mom describes the ordeal, she was "put in a 'cell' and left alone." The labor went on for twenty-four hours with no medication. Finally, Madeline was born, weighing nine and a half pounds. The baby had to be placed in an oxygen tent for the first twenty-four hours after birth. In those days women spent as much as two weeks in the hospital after giving birth. And in another couple of months my mother was pregnant again.

When Dad first started his electronic engineering business Mom knew about his police work; he was gone a lot of nights with

the vice squad. Mom was at the house when the FBI came look-
ing for the Brenda Allen recordings, so she knew about that mess
too. And my mother knew about Dad's work with Barney Ruditsky.
But about Mickey Cohen she knew nothing. She was never a part
of social times at Mickey's home. My parents' own social life was
spent with family. The reality was that my father was living two
very compartmentalized lives. And soon, into his life in organized
crime, there walked a whole new character.

14

A Date with Destiny

Syndicated crime was a bit of a journalistic term back in the 1940's. In reality each gambler worked in his own city in his own way. The big guns all knew each other alright, and they might borrow from one another in a pinch, like Siegel did from Meyer Lansky, paying for it with his life in the end. However, there was not usually a close business association between organized crime figures in different cities.

Be that as it may, St. Louis Andy was a friend of Mickey Cohen. As such, he strode into my father's office one day like a gangster out of a B movie. Andy was short and dark with a classic Brooklyn accent. His line to my father ran as follows: "Ya make lots of swell 'lectronic gadgets for Mickey, why doncha make a gadget so we can beat da wire service by a minute an' a half."

Andy's business was betting on the big horse races across the country. And like a good businessman he had thought of a way to beat the competition. He just needed a little help to pull it off.

Transfer your mind for a moment back to a time before mass communication as we know it today–very little television, no e-mail, no fax machines. The communication system for sending news across the United States was the wire service. The aspect Andy was interested in was the news of winning horses in various races across the nation. He figured if he could hold up the infor-

mation coming over the wire service for ninety seconds that would give him enough time to flash the winners to his cronies placing bets off-track in other parts of the country. Then they would let the information come through and clean up the cash every time.

You may recognize this as part of the plot line to the movie, *The Sting*, starring Robert Redford and Paul Newman. That's another movie I remember watching in the theater with my dad. When it got to the part where Redford and Newman were setting up their teletype equipment to beat the big time gambler, Lonegan, Dad spoke up loud enough for everyone around us to hear: "They stole my story!" In fact, the makers of the movie probably had "stolen" Dad's story, in the sense that they copied that part of the plot line, down to some minute details, from Dad's own movie, *Wiretapper*. That didn't stop my father from going back to see *The Sting* at least seven times in the theater, once for each of the Academy Awards won by the movie.

Back to the real story: Dad wasn't sure at first he could come up with a system to do what Andy wanted. He moonlighted at Andy's job for four months while still working for Cohen. Finally he came up with something he thought would work—a combination of teletype equipment and other electronic components. Andy and Dad tried out the system in Arizona; it worked like a charm. Andy was so elated he wanted to open up the business like a franchise all over the country.

Andy and my father were having a drink in a bar on Washington Boulevard in Los Angeles when Andy laid out his plan to go to St. Louis and set up Dad's electronic system to control the entire western half of the United States in illegal off-track betting. Andy doled out money and tickets to Dad and the other men for their meeting date in St. Louis–November 10, 1949.

My mother was nine months pregnant at the time, but my father was the one having trouble sleeping at night. My parents were about to bring a new life into the world but my father wasn't sure

he could properly account for what he had been doing with his own life. As Dad's date with destiny neared, he began to get edgier.

Sunday, November 6th started out as a gloomy day in every way. Whenever Dad made breakfast, culinary delights were not in the offing. He tried to help that morning but ended up burning the toast. Later, while playing ball with my sister, Madeline fell and scraped her foot.

My parents attended the worship service that Sunday morning at South Hollywood Pres. During the service the congregation sang the hymn "Pass Me Not O Gentle Savior." Looking at Dad during the singing, Mom could tell that he was somehow strangely moved.

After lunch my parents left Madeline with my mother's parents and headed to the funeral home to pay their respects to my father's Uncle Winfield who had died suddenly. As my parents exited the funeral parlor, my father's mood understandably darkened. In an attempt to lighten the day, my parents drove to the beach, but it was shrouded in fog.

On the way back Dad even stopped to see if Mickey Cohen was in, though he had never taken my mother by Mickey's home before, let alone mentioned his name. Mickey wasn't there, and that was unusual for him on a Sunday.

My parents went to a movie, *Pinky*, showing at Grauman's Chinese Theater in Hollywood. But that didn't help as the movie was a little too heart-searching—it only made my father think more deeply about his own troubled life.

My father made one more desperate attempt to lift the spirit of the day—he drove to the bar on Washington Boulevard where he usually met Andy and his buddies, but the place was so empty it echoed.

As my parents continued cruising along the streets of L. A., they came upon a tent meeting at the corner of Washington and Hill Streets where a hitherto unknown preacher by the name of Billy Graham was speaking. The newspapers had been closely covering

the canvas crusade because a number of celebrities had attended and had made public commitments to follow Jesus Christ. It was sufficiently interesting to newspaper magnate William Randolph Hearst to order all of his journalists to: "Puff Graham." The meeting was of particular interest to my father because an acquaintance of his, radio personality Stuart Hamblen, had recently "walked the sawdust trail" to the front of the tent.

The parking lot outside the tent on Hill Street was packed, but my parents decided to go into the meeting anyway, out of curiosity. When they entered, my father's mouth dropped open. It seemed like every one of the 6,500 seats were filled. It was standing room only in the big tent that night, but a few thoughtful people got up so my father and mother (obviously due to give birth at any moment) could sit down. It was still physically uncomfortable for Mom to sit on that hard seat.

Dad observed the crowd but had a hard time pinning a label on them, they were all so varied. He tried to keep his mental distance and find anything wrong that he could with the whole program. But when Graham stood up to speak, my father couldn't find any fault with him. That night Mr. Graham preached on the passage in the Gospel of Mark where Jesus queries: "For what shall it profit a man, if he shall gain the whole world, and lose his own soul?" (Mark 8:36)

When Graham gave the invitation, Dad watched as counselors singled out people, inviting them to "go forward" to the prayer tent and commit their lives to follow Christ. Dad flashed non-verbal "leave me alone" messages to everyone around. One of the counselors that night was a man known as "Uncle Billy" Scholfield. He gripped Dad's arm and was about to invite him forward when he saw the anger flashing in my father's eyes. Uncle Billy wisely bowed his head to pray. Then from the platform came the voice of Billy Graham once again: "There is a man in this audience, tonight, who has heard this message many times before, but he has never

given his life to Christ, and this may be his last opportunity." Dad sensed God speaking to him. For a moment he hesitated, suppressing his troubles and his own sense of need for a relationship with Christ. He had believed in God, and Jesus as God's Son, for all of his remembered life. Wasn't that nominal belief enough? Something in Graham's words, and in his own experience, convinced my father it wasn't enough. Without warning Dad whispered, "I'll go" and invited my mother to join him.

As Billy Graham later put it, "One evening when the Invitation was given, I noticed a giant of a man, tears rolling down his cheeks, coming up with his wife to receive Christ. I did not know who he was, but I asked Cliff to have the audience sing one more verse of the final song to give them time to reach the front."[4]

As my mother was recommitting her life to Christ, Dad knelt in the prayer tent and said, "God, if you'll mean business with me, I'll mean business with you. If you can take the tangled mess of my life and straighten it out, all I have is yours. I'll hold back nothing."

For the first time in his life Dad felt the "infinite abyss" inside him being filled with the "infinite and immutable" Spirit of God.

PART TWO:
Finding the Fullness
(1950-1957)

15

Making Headlines

My father had made the headlines in the newspapers on a number of occasions. Some of those headlines read: "Vaus in Custody after 'Hoax' on Vice Recordings Revealed" (*Los Angeles Examiner,* June 5 1949); "Bug Man Vaus Shows the Stuff that Nearly Blew Cohen to Kingdom Come" (*Los Angeles Daily News,* August 30, 1949).

But the headline in the *Los Angeles Times* on November 8, 1949 was perhaps the most startling: "Wire-Tapping Vaus Hits Sawdust Trail." And one of the headlines in another paper read: "Evangelist Converts Vaus, Sound Engineer in Vice Probe."

What had happened was this: as my parents left the tent meeting on November 6th, a newspaper photographer recognized my father and said, "Hey, Vaus, you've had your picture in the paper for everything else; how about letting us shoot a couple more and tell what happened here tonight?"

My father's first inclination was to turn the other way, but then he thought: What better way to tell the world of my newfound commitment? So my father consented to the photo shoot and the interview, thus sealing his new direction.

The morning of November 7, 1949, my father called Andy by long distance to tell him he wouldn't be in St. Louis on the tenth.

"What's da mattah? Ya crazy?" barked Andy. They argued back and forth for several minutes.

Andy pleaded, "Listen Jim, ya can't run out on me like dis, see? Who's gonna get da stuff set up and work it?"

"I don't know but I'm sure you'll find somebody."

"Dem kinda guys don't grow on trees. How long ya think it's gonna take us to get a guy like youse?"

Dad didn't answer. What could he say?

"The more I think of it, the less I like it, see? We got guys all over da place, costin' us dough. It's all outgo and no income till we get goin' on dis job. Either ya come to St. Louis or us guys is comin' to see youse."

But Dad's decision was final: "No Andy, I'm not coming to St. Louis."

"Den remember dis, no one quits on Andy. We'll be out to see ya."

That night my parents went back to the Billy Graham meeting. My mother started having labor pains while sitting in the tent. Mom timed the distance between labor pangs until, in the middle of the sermon, she said, "We've got to go!" A half-hour after they reached Hollywood Hospital, the same hospital where my mother had also entered the world, my brother Dennis was born, coincidentally on Billy Graham's birthday.

That night when Dad got home from the hospital the house was cold and all too quiet. Nana was taking care of Madeline so my father had the place to himself. He couldn't get Andy's words from that morning out of his mind. For the first time in his new-found Christian life Dad turned to the Bible for a glimmer of hope. Searching for something practical to help in his desperate time of need, he turned to the book of Proverbs. Scanning the pages his eyes lighted on Proverbs 16:7, "When a man's ways please the Lord, he maketh even his enemies to be at peace with him." Dad was betting his life on the truth of that verse.

On the third night my father went to the tent meeting, he was asked to come to the platform and talk about the decision he had made two nights before. In those early days it was difficult for my father to put into words what had happened to him. The glib religious phrases that had rolled off his tongue in church meetings long past were now gone. He simply stated that his life had not been all that it should have been and that from then on, he planned to live completely for the Lord. However, my father was only just beginning to learn what living completely for God was going to cost him.

16

Meeting with Andy

The day my father brought my mother and brother home from the hospital a big black sedan turned into their driveway in Baldwin Park. Several husky men piled out of the car, along with Andy. All my father could think of to say was, "Andy, you must have read the story of my change in the paper. What do you think?"

"I'll tell ya what I think. I think dat guy Graham give ya a couple a grand for standin' up and sayin' ya got religion. Now ya got your dough so let's get goin'. We got a job to do."

My father continued to try to explain to Andy what his new-found commitment to Christ really meant. Andy's guys looked at him like he was telling a bedtime story for little kids. For forty-five minutes Dad talked with Andy about the Lord until Andy's doubtful expressions turned to interest.

"Andy, why don't you come with me and hear for yourself? Come to the meeting tonight."

Andy tapped his foot nervously, "I would come, Jim, but I'm afraid."

"Afraid of what?"

"Afraid I might get what you got."

"That wouldn't be too bad, would it?"

"Maybe not, but I don't think I could live up to it."

"God will help you. He ..."

"Nope, it ain't for me. I got business. Let's go guys. So long, Jim." Andy's men turned, bewildered, then got in the car and they all drove away.

But that wasn't the last my father heard from St. Louis Andy. Dad began sharing his story whenever and wherever he had an invitation. One of those invitations came from Youth for Christ in San Diego. A couple of weeks later Dad received a long-distance phone call from Andy.

"Say Vaus, have you been down to San Diego shootin' off ya mouth?"

"Yes, Andy, I was telling people how Christ changed my life, just like I told you."

"Ya gotta cut dat out. Ya makin' me mad."

Andy raved on for several minutes until my father finally figured out what was wrong. Apparently Andy had located a guy to take Dad's place in the past-post betting operation. This man was an electronics engineer who lived in San Diego, but Andy enticed him to leave a well-paying respectable job with the telephone company and come to work for him. This man read in the San Diego Journal about my father speaking at the local Youth for Christ meeting. Since he knew of my father's previous connections with Andy, he wanted to hear what Dad had to say. After the meeting the man wrote to Andy: "I just want to tell you I've been to hear Jim Vaus and I've decided to quit before I even get started with you."

That was why Andy was fit to be tied. He threatened my father saying, "Ya gotta quit talkin' the way ya do. Ya costin' me a lot a dough."

"Andy, as long as I've got breath in my lungs, I'm going to keep telling people what Christ has done for me."

Andy banged down the receiver. On this occasion my father didn't even think twice about going back on his commitment to Christ, because in between Andy's visit and his phone call my father received some very important information.

One of the first groups to invite Dad to speak was the Christian Business Men's Committee (CBMC) in Hollywood. They met for breakfast at the Pig 'N Whistle on Hollywood Boulevard. After Dad spoke a woman stood up and said,

"Mr. Vaus doesn't know me, but I thought he would be interested in a report that came to me in the Mayor's office. A report came from the FBI saying that if Mr. Vaus had arrived according to schedule in St. Louis on November 10, he wouldn't have lived more than thirty minutes because a rival gang was set up to kill him."

That night in the Billy Graham meeting really was my father's last chance to commit his life to follow Jesus Christ.

17

Cutting Ties

After contacting St. Louis Andy, the next step for my father was to call on Mickey Cohen. Mickey couldn't understand why my father would come to his house early in the morning to tell him about Billy Graham. At first he thought Graham was a prizefighter, and he couldn't comprehend what my father was saying about becoming a Christian. Mickey was a Jew and he figured all Gentiles were already Christians. Dad tried to explain that you have to give your life to Christ; that is what makes a person a Christian. Mickey started to get an inkling of what my father was talking about and, amazingly, thought it was a beautiful thing. He said to my dad:

"Jim, I want you to make me a promise. Promise me you'll never go back to the old way of living. Hang on to what you've got. It's wonderful. A lot of guys aren't going to like it but if the whole world turns against you, remember there's one little Jew here that thinks the world of you for the decision you made and the guts you have to stand up for it."

Then Mickey went to his dresser and fished out a few thousand dollars in cash. My father only took what Cohen already owed him. "The Lord will take care of me," he said. Mickey really couldn't grasp that one, but he did want to meet Billy Graham.

Cohen and Graham met a few days later, along with my father and Cliff Barrows, at Mickey's house. Mickey had given the staff the night off. The four men hadn't been there together more than a half hour when the telephone rang. An Associated Press reporter was on the other end of the line hunting down a story. "Is it true that you are meeting with Billy Graham in your home right now?"

"No," came Mickey's thundering reply, "and if that guy ever showed up around here I wouldn't let him in anyway." Mickey hung up and turned to Graham, "You understand, Billy."

The meeting was a bit strained from that point on. Cohen wasn't quite sure how to entertain an evangelist in his home. Mickey offered drinks. Graham accepted a Coke. Then my dad and Billy Graham got down to business.

My father explained to Mickey, once again, how he had committed his life to follow Jesus Christ at the tent meeting, and the changes he planned to make. He tried to describe the peace and joy that had re-entered his heart. Then Mr. Graham explained the Good News about Jesus to Mickey as simply as he could.

Mickey responded with a few stories about his own life, especially noting the charitable organizations he had contributed to. Cohen told Graham that he respected him, and that he admired my father for the commitment he had made. Before Dad and Billy took their leave they had a prayer with Mickey. Then, as they were getting ready to go, suddenly Mickey started scurrying around looking for something. After peering into many cabinets and shelves, Cohen finally produced the object he had been hunting. It was a dust-covered Bible the Israeli government had sent him in gratitude for $300,000 Mickey had given in support of the Zionist movement. Apparently Mickey wanted my father, Billy and Cliff to know that he, too, had a Bible.

On the way to the door, Mickey and Billy planned their strategy should the AP reporter try to get a story out of either of them.

They agreed to stick to: "No comment." Sure enough, the reporter phoned Graham the next morning at dawn.

"I've been talking to Cohen and he says you were at his place last night. Is that true?"

Graham being a bit groggy, and not as experienced at handling interviewers as he would later become, responded: "If Mickey says so, it's true." The headline in the paper the next day read: "Wire-tapper In Confession As Evangelist Tries To Save Cohen."

18

Making Things Right with Men

One of the results of my father's conversion was that he not only wanted everything in his life to be right with God, but he wanted everything to be right with other people too. For my father this involved repaying everyone he had ever cheated or stolen from. At the close of that CBMC meeting at the Pig 'N Whistle in Hollywood, Dad called together several men to pray for him. He told them he had a list of about thirty people with whom he needed to make things right.

One of the first people on Dad's list was Don Bleitz, owner of the Bleitz Camera Company in Hollywood. Bleitz had clients in the motion picture industry as well as in private enterprise.

"Mr. Bleitz, I've come to bring back some stolen equipment. You probably had no idea what happened to this stuff, but do you remember ..." Dad proceeded to remind Don Bleitz of a time two years before when he received a purchase order from 20th Century Fox for a large quantity of equipment. Bleitz had delivered the equipment but had never received payment.

"I sure do remember. I reported it to the police once I realized it was a fake purchase order."

Dad continued, "I'm the man who stole it. I've brought back as much of it as I still have in my possession." My father went on to promise Don Bleitz that he would repay him for the equipment

he could not return as well as covering the cost of wear and tear on the stuff he did bring back.

Dad was relieved when Mr. Bleitz named the sum he would take to close the whole matter. Bleitz had no desire to press charges, but the cost of repayment put a significant dent in my parents' bank account. When Bleitz asked why my father was returning the equipment, Dad explained how he wanted to make his life right with God and with others. It was too simple for Bleitz to believe, but he was grateful for the repayment nonetheless.

Warner Brothers Broadcasting Corporation, Station KFWB, was another one on Dad's list. He wrote to them telling of how he had swindled their company and asked for an interview to arrange repayment. In response, Dad received this note in the mail:

Dear Mr. Vaus,

Your unusual but courageous letter of December 8th received and we are happy to note your admission and your change of attitude. That in itself is payment in full as far as we are concerned. With all best wishes for your future.

Cordially,

Harry Maizlish

General Manager

Next on my father's list was Dr. Louis T. Talbot, president of the Bible Institute of Los Angeles and pastor for seventeen years of the Church of the Open Door. When Dad was a student at Biola, he had taken money from Talbot's radio mail. In response to Dad's admission of guilt, Talbot urged him to "make his calling and election sure" and then forgave him.

Dad had never fully repaid the woman who had helped him to replace the stolen Biola yearbook funds. She had died before he could finish. Now he went back and put the balance in her estate.

From there it was on to the telephone company. They had been bothered so often by my father's wiretapping escapades they had assigned a special group of agents to catch my father in the act. Claude Peters was the chief of this group.

Dad piled a load of stolen telephone equipment in his car and drove to Peters' office. The secretary informed my father that Mr. Peters could not be disturbed. However, when Peters realized Jim Vaus was in the outer office, my father was ushered into Peters' presence without further ado.

"Vaus, it's a surprise to see you here. Tell me, is all I've been hearing about you true?"

"I don't know what you've heard, but if it was that I decided to follow Christ at a Billy Graham meeting, then yes, it's true. That's why I'm here."

"How's that?"

"I just wanted you to know I won't be tapping any more telephone lines and I have a car parked outside, loaded with telephone company equipment."

Peters sent some men outside to haul in the load. Once it was spread all over the floor of Peters' office he said, "Vaus, I think you really mean business." Then he proceeded to offer my father a job. Dad politely declined. He had given his life completely to Christ, for God's purposes, and at that point in time those purposes did not seem to include working for the telephone company.

Finally Dad arranged for a long delayed meeting with the Internal Revenue Service. My father had not reported the better part of his income for a couple of years. His Hollywood clients who had him do wiretapping didn't send him W-2 forms and Cohen paid in cash. In the end the IRS was more interested in what my father could tell them about Cohen's operations than they were in repayment.

Restitution was expensive in 1950's terms: $15,000 or more. My parents sold almost all of their worldly assets: car, house and furniture. When Dad had finished going through his restitution

list of thirty some odd people, he and Mom had nothing left but the clothes on their backs, but at least Dad was able to repay everyone who asked for it.

My parents had to move out of their home in Baldwin Park, along with Madeline and Dennis, in the spring of 1950. They were two days away from having to move and Dad was starting to worry. Mom said, "What are you worried about? We're supposed to be living one day at a time aren't we? And we don't have to move out for another two days! God will provide." Dad certainly could not have had a better partner in faith than Mom. Once the commitment to live for Christ was made, she was with Dad one hundred per cent and trusted God to bring them through every circumstance.

Riding the bus that day, Dad started memorizing a Bible verse that suddenly had new meaning to him. "Hitherto have ye asked nothing in my name: ask, and ye shall receive, that your joy may be full" (John 16:24). He had always thought of saying "in Jesus' name" at the end of his prayers as a way of saying goodbye to God. Now he began to pray in a different way. He asked for a house for his family in Jesus' name. And he began to believe that God would really do something.

Dad went to speak at a church in Sierra Madre that day. After the meeting a man named Pat Thornbury came up and shook Dad's hand.

"I was wondering if you needed a home," suggested Mr. Thornbury.

My father was dumbfounded. "What did you say?"

"I said: do you need a place to live?"

"Well, as a matter of fact I do." Dad admitted. "How much is the rent?"

"You don't understand," countered Mr. Thornbury, "I don't want to charge you rent; I want to give you a house to live in. My wife and I have just built a house in Whittier and we were planning to move in, but the Lord told me to give the house to you."

That was just the first of many "miracles." Consequently, from that point on in his life, my father often liked to quote the following poem by Martha Snell Nicholson:

One by one He took them from me,
All the things I valued most,
Until I was empty-handed;
Every glittering toy was lost.
And I walked earth's highways, grieving,
In my rags and poverty.
Till I heard His voice inviting,
"Lift your empty hands to me!"
So I held my hands toward heaven
And He filled them with a store
Of His own transcendent riches,
Till they could contain no more.
And at last I comprehended
with my stupid mind and dull
That God could not pour His riches
into hands already full![5]

19

From Perjurer to Truth-Teller

If paying back everyone from whom he had stolen seemed like a difficult task, it was nothing compared to what Dad realized he had to do next. My father recognized that he needed to change his false testimony in the Grand Jury trial that was in the process of railroading Sergeant E. V. Jackson to prison. My father went first to his attorney who told him he would have to make a choice between protecting his own skin or that of Sergeant Jackson. By changing his testimony my father was risking being put in prison for perjury. And if he didn't suffer from the law he might get it from Mickey Cohen's friends who had testified with him against Jackson.

Fully realizing what was at stake, Dad went home and wrote a long letter to the District Attorney; then he sent copies to each of the newspapers. Once again he hit the headlines of the Los Angeles Herald: "Wire-Tapper Confesses."

A day or two later my father was subpoenaed. On the appointed day, he arrived at the Hall of Justice and as the elevator door opened to the eighth floor he stepped into a mob of people. They were all waiting for the entertainment to start. Cameras flashed and reporters called out to him with a barrage of questions. As the trial was about to begin, Cliff Barrows and his father showed up. "Jim, we heard about the proceeding today and came to pray."

Dad took the witness stand, ready to come clean with the truth. The judge warned him that he didn't have to testify if his testimony would incriminate him. He further warned my father that if the evidence he was about to give was substantially the same as that in the papers the court would have no recourse but to return an indictment for perjury. Dad indicated that he wanted to continue under one condition, that he be allowed at the end of the proceeding to tell why he was changing his testimony.

The District Attorney fired questions at my father for the better part of the day. At the conclusion, Dad shared with the court that the reason for his change in testimony was due to his new commitment to follow Jesus Christ.

As soon as Dad finished speaking, the D. A. rose to his feet and queried, "Now Vaus, since you got religion ..."

"I didn't say I'd got religion."

"Well, since you've seen the light."

"I didn't say anything about seeing any light."

"Well then, since you hit the sawdust trail."

"I didn't mention a sawdust trail."

"Well then, what did you say?"

"I said that I had decided to follow Jesus Christ."

The District Attorney sat down again and that ended the proceeding. Sergeant E. V. Jackson was exonerated of all charges. A short time later Dad received the following letter from Sergeant Jackson:

Dear Mr. Vaus,

Your recent testimony concerning the case involving me deserves more gratitude than I am able to express. It was comforting to suddenly find the truth present when I had been surrounded for a number of months by distortions of fact and complete falsehoods.

Your decision to correct your past statements regardless of the consequent action against you reflects a strong desire on your part to right a wrong. The courage shown by doing this is commendable,

and it is most unusual to find a person who will jeopardize his liberty for the sake of truth.

I hope and believe that there will be no action against you, although I have not discussed it with anyone of authority. I thank you and wish you well.

Sincerely,

E. V. Jackson

My father was never indicted for perjury and other miracles continued to happen on a daily basis. When my parents were down to five dollars in the bank and they needed groceries, the tab would come to $4.89. When the car was running on empty, a friend at church would just "happen" to slip some cash into my father's hand. When the car was gone, people provided rides. It was hard for Dad to accept so many helping hands; it wounded his pride. But he learned to say thank you. And he also learned who was really in control.

20

No Turning Back

There were times when my father must have been tempted to turn back to his old way of life-like the time Mickey Cohen offered to buy Dad a car. My father turned him down. Cohen questioned, "But Jim, how are you going to get around?" And Dad responded, "The streetcars are still running."

Then there was the time Dad was offered a large sum of money for a certain wire recording he had in his possession, a recording of two California politicians. In his old wiretapping days when he didn't have anything else to do, he would listen in on various telephone conversations from his office in Hollywood. That's how he came by the recording of the California politicians.

A Washington newspaper reporter who had made some remarks about one of the politicians in question was being sued for defamation. The reporter believed that my father's recording would prove his statements to be true and make his case for him. The reporter sent a hireling to California to try to obtain these tapes from Dad, but the hired hand went about his work in a circuitous manner. He joined one of the most well known churches in Los Angeles in order to put up a religious front to my father. Then he looked Dad up.

"I'm glad to meet you, Jim. I am looking forward to getting to know you now that we belong to the same church."

"Which church is that?" my father questioned.

The man named the church.

"I'm not a member of that church."

The reporter's hireling was clearly frustrated. Getting to know Dad through the church connection was clearly the focal point of his strategy. Since that didn't work the man offered my father a straight $10,000 for the recordings.

Dad shot back at him, "Evidently you haven't heard."

"Haven't heard what?"

"Jim Vaus is dead."

The man's eyes bugged out, his jaw dropped. He must have thought he was speaking to a ghost.

"That's right," my father continued, "The man you were looking for, the one who used to do wiretapping and sell the recordings to the highest bidder, that man is dead. I'm a new man. It's like the Bible says, 'If any man be in Christ, he is a new creature.'" That stopped the reporter's hired hand for a couple of days. Then he called on my father again, this time with a new angle.

"Jim, I've been talking to my boss in Washington. He says I never should have offered you that $10,000. He knows you are a changed man; he so enthusiastically approves of the work you are doing he would like to build a church for you."

Dad wearily responded, "Thank your boss for his interest, but I'm sure if God wants me to build a church he will provide the money for it."

That settled the matter for another three or four days until Dad received a phone call from a prominent criminal lawyer in Los Angeles. He insisted that my father come to his office. Dad had been in trouble so many different ways he figured he better see what the whole business was about, so he went to the attorney's office.

When he arrived the lawyer acted as the spokesperson for several gentlemen who were gathered in his office.

"Vaus, we are so glad to hear about the great work you have been doing for the Lord. We have heard wonderful reports about your preaching in churches."

"Thanks," my father said skeptically. At that point in time he had only shared his story in front of a few audiences.

The attorney continued, "We think what you are doing is so great, we'd like to finance you to take your message on the road. We'll buy everything you need–tents, chairs, organ, whatever!"

"Since when are you guys so interested in evangelism?"

"Well now, Vaus, you know us."

"Of course I know you. That's why I'm asking. What's the catch?"

"No catch," mumbled the lawyer, "Naturally, you might be able to help us with something. You do have a certain wire recording ..."

"So that's it. Well, I know all about the wire recording. But I guess you guys haven't heard."

At that point a guy in the back of the room piped up, "Yeah, yeah, we know, we know, you're dead! You're dead!"

Dad stood up, and trying to help them understand, echoed the Apostle Paul, "It's because the old Jim Vaus was crucified with Christ."

Every one of those men in the lawyer's office gave my father blank stares. But that didn't matter to Dad, he just walked out. He was getting good at walking out on people when he needed to.

21

Right Place, Right Time

After my father's conversion made the papers he began to have numerous invitations to share with groups of people how Jesus Christ had changed his life. One of the first invitations was to speak at a Youth for Christ meeting at the Municipal Auditorium in Minneapolis. I believe George Wilson, who later became the manager of the Billy Graham Evangelistic Association offices in Minneapolis, arranged the invitation. Nothing could have adequately prepared my father for stepping on that stage on December 10, 1949, just one month after his conversion, and relating his life story to a sea of some ten thousand faces.

After Minneapolis my father received yet another historic invitation, this time to join Billy Graham on the platform at his next crusade in Boston at the beginning of 1950. Dad immediately promised Billy he would be there.

Shortly after the phone call from Mr. Graham, Dad heard from the Youth for Christ office in Los Angeles. They had been scheduling meetings for him and the secretary said, "I noticed you had no meetings scheduled for January so I told a church in Gardena that you would lead two weeks of meetings for them."

"You'd better cancel it, Helen," my father retorted, "I have never spoken for more than one night. I'd have a hard time coming up

with talks for two nights, let alone two weeks. Besides, Billy Graham has asked me to join him in Boston in January. I just can't do it." In Dad's mind, that settled it.

During those early days following his conversion, my father began to read the Bible and pray every morning before starting the day. One morning he prayed, "Lord, I'll go wherever you want me to go." Immediately the Gardena meetings popped into his mind, but he tried to forget about it; he wanted to be in Boston with Billy. Still, every time Dad prayed he couldn't keep Gardena out of his mind. Finally, he made a compromise with the Lord: "I'll go to Gardena if Helen hasn't cancelled the meetings."

Dad called Helen. She apologized for having forgotten to cancel the meetings. So my father called the pastor himself. The pastor explained how my father had been in their church to speak a couple of weeks before and they had a prayer meeting following that. As a result, the leadership of the church decided they wanted to have two weeks of evangelistic meetings. They didn't want fancy sermons; they were willing to settle for whatever the Lord put on Dad's heart. So my father finally relented.

There was just one problem: Dad had no convenient form of transportation to get to Gardena. When he had earlier run out of money, he told the finance company where to pick up his old car, and it could take five hours on the streetcar to get to and from Gardena every day.

About this time Dad realized there was one more person with whom he needed to get right—Dawson Trotman, founder of the Navigators ministry. Dad had met Trotman while he was a student at Biola, back at the time Dad was talking the Christian talk but not walking the walk. Trotman, after hearing Dad's so-called Christian testimony, called him a phony to his face. That aroused bitterness in Dad toward Daws, a bitterness he couldn't shake. Whenever someone mentioned Trotman's name, my father made unkind remarks about him.

Having gotten right with God, Dad realized the way he had responded to Daws' rebuke was not right. He went to Trotman's office and apologized. Trotman was shocked at first but then he and my father patched things up and became fast friends.

When Daws heard about Dad's meetings in Gardena he queried: "How are you going to get there?"

"By the streetcar," Dad replied.

"I think I can help you," said Daws. After that, Trotman assigned an assortment of people from the Navigator staff to drive my parents to and from Gardena every day for the entire two weeks of meetings. Later, Daws helped Dad to get a car of his own.

The meetings in Gardena were incredible. Many times after being dismissed at 9 pm, people hung around and just wouldn't go home. Reports came from the prayer room of people accepting Christ and others rededicating their lives to follow the Lord. Before the two weeks were finished the men of the church had to knock out a wall to accommodate the crowds who were coming. The church expanded from a 75-seat auditorium to one that would seat 475 people.

Not long after the Gardena meetings, Dad returned home one day to find a car parked out in front of the house. The man behind the wheel called out, "Hey Vaus, we'd like to talk with you for a few minutes." The man flashed his FBI credentials, so Dad got in the car with him and his fellow officer.

"We have some bad news for you. We have orders from Washington to place you under arrest."

"What for?" my father asked incredulously.

"Armed robbery."

For a second my father felt as he had years before when he was arrested at the Broadway Department Store under the same charge, but nothing was making sense this time. "Where was this robbery?" he queried further.

"In Boston Massachusetts—you were there on January 17th weren't you?"

"Where exactly?"

"The Brink's express office."

Dad had read in the paper about the Brink's Boston express office robbery that had taken place on January 17, 1950. The Brink's operation was supposedly burglar proof. However, some men in Halloween masks had knocked them over for a small fortune amounting to several million dollars.

"The guys in Washington seem to think you are one of the few guys who could have planned a job like this. You were in Boston at that time, weren't you?"

"No, as a matter of fact I wasn't," Dad replied with a sense of satisfaction. "If you will look in my date book here you will see that Boston is crossed out for those dates and Gardena is put in its place. I was supposed to be with Billy Graham in Boston, but I had a prior commitment at a little church in Gardena."

The FBI officers asked a few more questions, but that was it. They drove away and my father never heard from them again. That incident taught my father the importance of being wherever the Lord wanted him to be–at all times!

22

On the Road Again

To make up for not being in Boston with Billy Graham in January 1950, my father did appear on the platform with him during a crusade held in the summer of that same year in Portland, Oregon. It was in Portland that Mr. Graham decided to begin a radio program called *The Hour of Decision*. The program debuted on November 5, 1950 during Graham's subsequent crusade in Atlanta, and my father played an interesting role in Graham's first radio broadcast.

Back in those early days, Mr. Graham moved around the platform quite a bit. My father thought he might have a gimmick that would free up Graham in the presentation of his message; it was a wireless microphone. The mike clipped on to Graham's tie, the power unit was attached to his belt and the antenna was hidden, running down the inside of his pant leg. Graham liked the idea of being set free from entangling microphone cords so he was willing to try this new invention for his first radio broadcast.

Unfortunately, in the middle of Graham's sermon the rubber tip at the end of the antenna wire came off. So every time the exposed tip hit his leg, which it did a lot during the course of the sermon, it gave him an electric shock.

My father always maintained that no one was more gracious, both in public and in private, than Billy Graham. But that night

when Mr. Graham came off the platform he gave my father a piece of his mind. He marched my father back to the dressing room and told him off in no uncertain terms. Dad was understandably discouraged. But the next morning my father found a note slipped under his hotel room door. "Please forgive me for my anger. I couldn't love you more if you were my own brother. Billy."

Dad started having so many invitations to speak in churches, prisons, schools and other venues across the country that home became a stopping place between trips. So in September 1950, through the help of J. Paul Getty, my parents purchased a thirty-three foot Spartan trailer. This made it possible for them to be together more, and allowed Dad to accept the speaking invitations he was receiving.

My father had repeated his conversion story so many times it began to sound like a broken record. To refresh his message he used electronics as a tool to expose the unseen and unheard immanence of God. He eventually had help hauling about two tons of electronic equipment around the country for use in his meetings. With ultraviolet and black light Dad could show the brilliant colors hidden in a grey granite slab of rock.

Black light of course picks up many things unseen in ordinary light. One of those is lipstick traces. Dad enjoyed both amazing and embarrassing young people with that black light. On one occasion he told a young man in front of a college audience all about the date he had the night before. The college student had parked in a car and the girl sat on his right. Dad declared that the girl had kissed him, not once, but many times over. How was Dad so sure? Although the young man's face appeared clean under normal lighting conditions, the black light revealed the pigment of die from the lipstick still in the pores of the young man's skin. The sight of that college student's face under the black light brought a roar of laughter from the audience. It was a great way to begin a talk about how no one can hide from the eyes of God.

Percy Crawford was a friend of my father who invited him to speak on a number of occasions. Crawford had come to faith in Christ at Church of the Open Door in Los Angeles and gone on to study for the ministry at Biola, Wheaton, Princeton and Westminster Seminary. Crawford, an evangelist to the core, became a pioneer in Christian radio and television broadcasting, founded Pinebrook Bible Conference in the Pocono Mountains of Pennsylvania, and later, King's College in Briarcliff Manor, New York.

On one occasion when my father was speaking at Pinebrook, the leaders were having a problem with a camper who was stealing. The real difficulty was that they couldn't seem to catch the young person in the act. Dad told the camp officials he had a solution. He spread some invisible powder on some bills and then left the money in a place where the thief was bound to find it. Sure enough, the next time the camp leaders checked the location, the money was gone.

That night in the camp meeting, before Dad began his message, he explained to everyone in the audience that there was a thief in their midst. He promised that the camp leadership would go easy on the thief if he would quietly slip out of his seat and meet the camp counselors who were waiting for him in the foyer of the auditorium. Dad warned the young criminal that if he didn't take the chance right now to confess his guilt, he would be exposed during the course of the meeting.

No one moved. Dad continued with his talk, going through the audience and explaining how black light reveals things normally hidden to the human eye. When he came to the young man who had stolen the money the black light made it quite obvious. The invisible powder on the bills had left marks all over the young man's hands, which then transferred to his clothing and face. All of this was revealed by the unforgiving black light. The thief was exposed and the audience got the point: you can't hide from God, so why not confess your sin to God before it is too late.

The discussion periods following Dad's talks were often very fruitful spiritually. Young people especially enjoyed talking to my father after his meetings. He wasn't a priest in an ivory tower who couldn't understand what they were going through. Rather, he was a man who had known many struggles in his young life, just as his listeners experienced. He was fairly un-shock-able, so people of all ages felt comfortable talking to him about their problems. His life gave them hope.

23

The Long, Long Trailer

While Dad's public speaking ministry was bearing fruit for eternity, life for my parents in the trailer wasn't easy. Dad often had to leave Mom, Madeline and Dennis behind when they couldn't make it fast enough with the trailer to Dad's next appointment. My father would have to take a plane to his next stop while my mother, sister and brother would stay behind in a strange trailer park.

One of those trailer parks was near a Baptist college in Springfield, Missouri. Jean Haldeman was one of the residents in the park; her husband was a student at the college. Jean thought my mother should develop a little bit of independence and learn how to drive, so she taught her during the two or three weeks Mom spent in Springfield.

From Springfield it was on to Atlanta for the Billy Graham meetings and from there my parents drove to Philadelphia. It was in Philadelphia that my father started using black light as part of his presentation, but he had trouble at first. After one of the meetings, Dad woke up in the middle of the night; the inside of his eyelids felt like sandpaper. When he tried to open his eyes he couldn't. Mom had to drive Dad to the hospital. He wasn't sure which was scarier, being blind or Mom driving him! The blindness turned out

to be a temporary problem resulting from looking at the black light for too prolonged a period of time.

There were numerous mishaps while my parents were criss-crossing the country in the long, long trailer. One time my brother Dennis ate a jar of cold cream while they were on the road. Dennis and Madeline were always falling out of bed. Another time while my parents were driving up a long, gradual incline, the trailer suddenly unhitched at the top of the hill. Thankfully, it didn't crash into anyone on its descent.

After the meetings in Philadelphia, my parents drove to Cleveland where Dad had more meetings. Then it was on to Chicago, where they were joined by my mother's sister, Helen, who flew from Los Angeles to keep my mother company. After Dad's meeting in Bloomington, cold weather was setting in, so he felt they should drive as far south as they could that night. They drove through the gloomy streets of Chicago and then out of the city until they came to a bridge. They started across and then the car started to fishtail on the ice. The trailer swung completely around pushing them head-on into another vehicle. Amazingly, Dennis and Madeline, who were asleep in the back seat, were not awakened by the accident. Fortunately the damage to the car and trailer was minor so that my parents were able to continue on their way the next day.

In a couple of days they finally did reach a warmer climate in Oklahoma, where they stopped beside the road to sleep. "Oklahoma, where the wind comes whistling down the plain!" The winds were so bad that night that Aunt Helen had finally had enough; she wanted to get back to Southern California as quickly as she could. Dad drove her to the airport that night and put her on a plane.

Dad left Mom and kids, once again in a trailer park, this time in Roswell, New Mexico, while he went on to meetings in Great Falls, Montana. My mother was encouraged during this time by Paul's statement in Philippians 4:11, "...for I have learned, in what-

soever state I am, therewith to be content." Mom learned how to be content in the state of New Mexico, Oklahoma, Missouri, Illinois, or wherever she was!

My parents got home to California in time to spend Christmas with both of their families. But in January Dad set out, alone again. There was no point in hauling the trailer through winter weather anymore. So Mom, Madeline and Dennis stayed in the trailer, parked on Aunt Betty and Uncle Lester's property in warm San Fernando Valley.

There were many times during the 1950's when my parents were apart from each other due to my father's work. But they often had fun reunions–like the time one Christian group that had invited my father to speak had my mother flown back east to surprise him at the meeting. In *This is Your Life* fashion, they brought a large box out in front of my father on stage–and who should pop out of it but my mother!

In 1951 Dad had his first book published, *Why I Quit Syndicated Crime*, with the profit to go to the work of The Navigators. In June, my parents set out together again in the trailer, this time heading north. Two Navigators, Don Hardy and Ken Nanfelt traveled with them in a separate station wagon hauling Dad's electronic equipment. Every nook and cranny of the trailer was packed with copies of Dad's book. The only consolation for my mother was that as they journeyed from town to town Dad sold books in each place, thus making more room for the family in the trailer.

When Dad spoke in Molalla, Oregon he asked Mom to say a word from the microphone. And that was all she was able to get out ... one word ... hello! In Yakima, Washington, Dad scheduled Mom to speak to a women's group. She did better there, even though she was speaking to over five hundred women on the Yakima Fair Grounds. She shared from her heart how the Lord had been her strength through all of their travels. "My grace is sufficient for thee: for my strength is made perfect in weakness" (2 Corinthians 12:9).

From Yakima my parents drove on to Seattle where Mom, yet again, stayed alone in a trailer park while Dad flew on to meetings in Alaska. When Dad returned, they journeyed down the west coast together and my father continued speaking in various venues along the way.

By the time they reached Los Angeles my parents had been traveling in the trailer off and on for a year. And by that time my parents were expecting their third child; it was time to settle down in a regular home again. The Lord provided just the right place for them to live–the house my father grew up in at 945 East Edgeware Road in Los Angeles. My parents bought the house from Grandpa Jim and Grandma Lillie and moved in their few belongings in October 1951.

It was there that my father received a surprise in the mail: a subpoena to testify against Mickey Cohen. Cohen was charged with tax evasion and my father was one of a hundred or more witnesses whom the court hoped could nail Mickey. Dad didn't want to hurt Mickey in any way, but he told the truth about what he knew; it wasn't much. Still, Cohen was sentenced to five years; he served three and a half of those years at McNeil Island Federal Penitentiary, one of the places where Dad had been imprisoned. When Cohen was released from jail, Dad's insurance company got nervous about how Mickey might repay those who had testified against him, so they cancelled my father's accidental death insurance. Sometimes telling the truth just doesn't seem to pay ... at least in worldly terms.

24

A Year of Blessings and Challenges

*W*hy *I Quit Syndicated Crime* was actually written by a ghost writer, Dorothy Haskin, not by my father. Dad was too active to ever sit down and write a book all on his own. And he didn't read many books either; it is even questionable how carefully he proofread *Why I Quit Syndicated Crime* before it went to press. Though the book is substantially accurate, it does not sound the way my father spoke. And that is just the point–my father was a speaker, not a writer.

Be that as it may, *Why I Quit Syndicated Crime* must have been a very popular book. I don't know how many copies were actually sold. However, one copy of the British edition, which I have in my possession, indicates ten printings from 1956 to 1973. The American edition had a similar amount of printings, almost one per year, starting in 1951. The book was also translated into several foreign language editions. Those I have in my possession include: Swedish (1961), German (1962 & 1963), French (1965), Italian (1965), Spanish (1982), as well as an edition for English speaking Asia (1978). I was even told, by Dr Peter Kuzmic of Yugoslavia, about a bootleg copy of my father's book which was translated, printed and distributed behind the Iron Curtain.

In 1952, Dorothy Haskin ghost wrote another book, this time for my mother, entitled: *They Called My Husband a Gangster*. This book too went into a number of printings throughout the 1950's. However, just as *Why I Quit Syndicated Crime* doesn't sound like my father, *They Called My Husband a Gangster* really does not sound like my mother. Still, over the years my mother has received numerous letters from people who have been led into a personal relationship with Jesus Christ through reading "her" book, and for that she is grateful.

My mother must have been very busy in 1952, not only with the publication of her book, but also with the birth of my brother Steve in April at Good Samaritan Hospital. Mom barely had time to get home from the hospital and get settled before the doctors told my parents that my older brother, Dennis, would need eye surgery. Dennis has suffered from a "lazy eye" which was not completely corrected by the surgery he underwent in July 1952, at two years and eight months of age. The hospital stay was a traumatic experience for my brother who still remembers his hands being tied to the bars of the crib by medical personnel.

Amazingly, while my brother Dennis was being operated on, my father was not present. It is hard to understand why my father would not be there for such a critical event in his child's life. If my child was being operated on, wild horses couldn't keep me away from the hospital. Without excusing my father's neglect of his family, it must be recognized that life was very different in the 1950's from what it is today. Women were given the sole duty of tending the home fires, while men went to work. My father's work at that time involved a lot of travel, similar to a traveling salesman, a trucker, or other lines of work which might take a man away from his home. In addition, my father was riding the crest of a wave that started with the 1949 Billy Graham meetings in Los Angeles. Graham was catapulted to national attention by those meetings, and so was my father. Though Mr. Graham's schedule was perhaps

more demanding than Dad's, they each were seizing every opportunity they had to reach people for Christ. Billy Graham admits today that he traveled too much, he accepted too many invitations, and he neglected his family. The same was true of my father, and perhaps if he were alive today he would be the first to admit it.

On July 18, 1952, Dad was ordained by the arrangement of Torrey Johnson, then pastor of the Midwest Bible Church in Chicago. Among the forty-one ministers who participated in Dad's ordination were: Louis T. Talbot, President of Biola, Charles T. Cook, editor of *The Christian*, London, England, H. A. Hermansen, Pastor of Moody Memorial Church, Claude A. Ries, Professor, Houghton College, R. L. Decker, Executive Director of the National Association of Evangelicals, Wendell P. Loveless, the hymn-writer and pastor of Wheaton Evangelical Free Church, and my grandfather, James A. Vaus, Sr. George Beverly Shea sang "Little Is Much When God Is in It" and Torrey Johnson delivered the message.

After this trip, which included speaking engagements at military bases where he gave away hundreds of books, Dad was so anxious to get home, he drove practically non-stop from Maryland to Los Angeles. The day after his arrival he was absolutely wiped out. While moving some of his heavy equipment around the garage Dad's knees buckled. He knew something more than fatigue was plaguing him for he was suddenly paralyzed from the waist down. His doctor said it was polio. Sister Kenny, a very kind woman who had dedicated her life to the rehabilitation of polio victims, confirmed this diagnosis at the El Monte Hospital. She told my father he might walk after a year, but that he would, most likely, walk with a limp for the rest of his life.

My father had received little remuneration for his speaking engagements that year. When he came down with polio, my parents were down to nothing in the bank. Feeling overwhelmed and discouraged, Dad searched the Scriptures for comfort and guidance. At that time, it was Jeremiah 12:5 that touched him: "If thou hast

run with the footmen, and they have wearied thee, then how canst thou contend with horses?" Dad was challenged by that verse to present his problem to the Lord in prayer. Within days, a partial answer to that prayer came in the mail: a $700 check from Stuart Hamblen and his wife.

Still, Dad felt there was no way he could go on with his planned speaking engagements for the latter half of 1952. The one he was most disappointed to cancel was an invitation to speak at Moody Memorial Church in Chicago. The meeting was only four weeks away so Mom wrote a note to cancel. Within four days my father received the following telegram from the leaders of Moody Church: "We believe God will take care of you, continuing to advertise your series. See you then." Billy Graham got word of Dad's condition and asked people listening to *The Hour of Decision* to pray for him.

Dad didn't leap out of the hospital bed kicking his heels, but he did have a rapid recovery. In less than a month he was home, and a few days later he was loaded, wheelchair and all, on a plane bound for Chicago. When he landed in Illinois my father was too embarrassed to use the wheelchair, so with some difficulty he walked off the plane. When he stood up to speak at Moody Church that week, all four thousand seats were filled.

25

To All The World

Dad was influenced by Billy Graham in many ways. In the early days of his ministry he established the Jim Vaus Evangelistic Association, patterning his own organization after that of Mr. Graham. However, Dad's organization took on a different twist from Graham's; it became a nonprofit corporation in support of a second one: Missionary Communication Service (MCS), incorporated in Washington DC in June 1953.

The goal of MCS was to put missionaries in isolated corners of the world in touch with others who could help and encourage them in their ministries. The same electronics expertise Dad had used in service of the syndicate and lately to communicate the gospel more effectively to the masses would now be used for the purpose of global missions, mostly in Africa and South America. It was the design of MCS to bear the cost of equipment–including transmitters, receivers and generators. Mission boards, in turn, would pay nominal maintenance and repair costs after the equipment was installed. There was a building in western New York that would house the large stateside transmitting and receiving station. This installation was to handle communications and voice conversations between overseas points and the United States.

My father gathered an interesting collection of men to be on the board of MCS including V. Raymond Edman, President of Wheaton College; William Nyman, Secretary and Treasurer of the Wycliffe Bible Translators; Clyde Taylor, Secretary of Affairs, National Association of Evangelicals; and Dawson Trotman, President and Founder of the Navigators and member of the Billy Graham team.

The communication system Dad designed was used, among other things, to transmit medical advice to missionary outposts where doctors were scarce. Doctors would listen to missionaries describe symptoms of patients over the airwaves and then prescribe medicines for the diseases they had diagnosed. Doctors could also coach midwives in remote villages in the process of delivering babies. Furthermore, the communication system provided news and information and contact with families for missionaries who otherwise would have felt cut off from the world.

MCS gave Dad a project into which he was able to funnel the surplus money he began receiving from his speaking engagements. By the mid 1950's, our family was well provided for, as Dad was receiving thousands of dollars per month. So my father wanted to share what he could with other Christians in need.

Putting communication systems into remote villages was the easy thing. The hard part was getting there. Dad always said the most difficult part of his travel for MCS was the last fifty miles. After my father had gone as far as he could by plane, he would hop aboard whatever form of transportation was available. In Yarinacocha, Peru, that transportation was a dugout canoe. When Dad moved his then 300-pound body into the boat, it almost sank the little vessel. Another quarter of an inch and he would have been swimming. What a sight: a blue-eyed, white man, dressed in a business suit in a canoe in South America!

When he arrived at the village, Dad received a meal that he could not identify but he was afraid to ask what it was. He was then assigned a grass hut on stilts to sleep in. His bed was a sleeping bag

and a bunch of mosquito netting. By this time in his life Dad was accustomed to appearing before large crowds, but nothing could have prepared him for the crowd he drew that night. The villagers surrounded the hut and peeked through the slats. What was the attraction? They had never seen a white man that big, and they wanted to get a look at him naked. Dad did his best to disappoint the villagers, changing his clothes as quickly as possible and then diving into his sleeping bag. As he did so the grass hut rustled.

My father kept MCS going until 1957, but the financial difficulties that had plagued the organization all along became too much to manage. Though money from his speaking engagements established the work, and the revenues from his first book were channeled to MCS, it still wasn't enough to meet the need. The work that Dad started was eventually given to Missionary Aviation Fellowship in California. That organization very ably combined communications and aviation for missionaries. MAF continues the communication arm of their service to this day with MAF Link.

26

Judge or Jester?

At a very young age my father's family nicknamed him Judge. Perhaps it was because he could get a particular expression on his face that made him look "as sober as a judge." My father certainly had his serious side, but he could be a barrel of laughs as well.

On one occasion when Dad was in Minneapolis he visited the Billy Graham Evangelistic Association offices. After his meeting there he invited a group of the secretaries to go out to lunch with him. They all accepted delightedly. As they were on their way walking out of the building, the ladies were walking in front of my father. One secretary said to another, "You know, I think I've really lost some weight recently." Quick as a wink, with his hands on his stomach, Dad quipped, "I think I found it!"

One of Dad's funniest stories from life on the road was about a time he spoke at Wheaton College. Every year the graduating class put on a party that was "the" event on the school calendar. One year they invited my father to be their speaker, but it was a big secret, with his identity being known to only one or two people on the planning committee.

This senior party was a very fancy affair and so Dad had ordered a tuxedo. As usual, my father was on a tight schedule and flew into Chicago the day of the event. He went to Ginges Brothers to try on

the tux, but the guy who wore it before him must have been bigger around and much shorter. The tailor said there was plenty of material so that he could easily lengthen the trousers. Dad was staying with the Van Kampens who ran Van Kampen Press, the publishers of his first book. He asked the tailor to get the altered tux to the Van Kampen's house in time for him to change clothes and get over to the college. The tailor assured my father that the tux would be at the Van Kampen's house, some twenty-five miles away, in time for him to get ready for the event that evening.

When Dad arrived at the house later that day, he asked Mrs. Van Kampen if his tux had been delivered. Much to my father's relief, she told him that it had and she handed him the package. He opened the box and found the shirt, tie and everything apparently in good order. He had only minutes to spare so he hurriedly dressed. But as he slipped on the pants Dad realized that instead of lengthening the trousers by eight to ten inches, the tailor had shortened them that much. The pant cuffs were just below his knees.

What was my father to do? He had only minutes before he had to be on the Wheaton College campus. He had to have formal wear for this dress occasion. There was no other alternative. He had to make this tux work somehow. Dad found that as he stood before the mirror he could lower the pants to a level that looked alright with the coat buttoned. The cuffs were just above his ankles but maybe no one would notice. After all, this was a dinner event. Maybe it would be dark. Dad figured he would give it a go.

Minutes later my father showed up at the Wheaton College gymnasium. The students had done a wonderful job decorating. They had transformed the gym into a medieval castle. Dad's liaison from the planning committee met him at the door and said, "This is terrific. No one knows you are the guest of honor and it is going to be a wonderful surprise."

Then the liaison explained to my father, "Wait right here by the door. When the musicians blow their trumpets you are to enter

the gym on this red carpet. Then walk the length of the gym to the place where you will be sitting next to the king and queen."

Dad waited for the trumpet blast and then started his long trek down the red carpet. But about half way down the carpet the pants started to go, and with every step they slipped an inch further. With his inimitable sense of humor my father decided to play court jester. He locked his knees together and waved as he went. The audience came unglued and roared with laughter. Dad barely made it to his table before losing the pants completely. He hurriedly sat down while the crowd continued to clap. As he adjusted his pants he explained to those at his table the predicament he was in. I'm sure they all tried to cover for him as best they could.

When Dad was at Wheaton again a couple of years later, he told the story of what happened that night at the senior party. He could hardly quiet the crowd for the gales of laughter that erupted.

27

Wiretapper: The Movie

In 1954, Dick Ross and Great Commission Films made a feature length movie about my father's life and conversion, based upon his best-selling book, *Why I Quit Syndicated Crime*. *Wiretapper* had one of the largest budgets ever to be appropriated for a Christian motion picture up to that time. The movie, starring Bill Williams as my father and Georgia Lee as my mother, premiered at the Shrine Auditorium in Los Angeles during the last week of April 1955. Admission was free. My father spoke at the premiere and gave an invitation for people to commit their lives to follow Christ. One hundred and twenty-five people came forward to the platform that night to register their decision to follow Jesus Christ.

As I mentioned in the preface, my father always thought the movie was a little bit on the corny side, but it received attention in national magazines like *Life*, and a good review in *Time* magazine. *Time* (April 25, 1955) described *Wiretapper* as "the latest and possibly most potent weapon in the arsenal of a personable young evangelist."[6] As *Time* also noted, all of the proceeds from the film went directly to furthering the ministry of Missionary Communication Service.

Wiretapper has been viewed by countless people all around the world; it is available today on video cassette from World Wide Pictures or you can even watch it online at www.billygraham.org. One man's story is typical of the response to the film. Alec Rowlands saw the *Wiretapper* as a young man in South Africa. As a result, he committed his life to follow Jesus Christ. Years later, in one of those divine arrangements of life, Alec, and his wife Rita, came to work with my father in ministry.

In typical Hollywood fashion there are many things in the *Wiretapper* that were changed from real life. Names were changed to protect the innocent and the guilty. And the dramatic scene where Dad disarms the bomb at the mobster's house while my mother was giving birth to my sister, Madeline, didn't exactly happen that way. My father did disarm a bomb at Mickey Cohen's house, but that was not at the same time as my sister's birth, which my father was present to witness.

Despite the fact that Bill Williams looked nothing like my father, and Georgia Lee's portrayal was far more syrupy-sweet than my mother, the *Wiretapper* still has an impact. The acting is melodramatic to say the least, but the amazing thing is that as the movie nears its climax the message really comes through. Perhaps the film is worth watching just to see what Billy Graham was like in his early days. His preaching was loud, fast-paced and dramatic. Though that style may not be suited to today's audiences, I have still seen it have a positive effect on people with whom I have watched *Wiretapper* over the past twenty years or so.

One more thing about the movie should be mentioned. There is a scene in the film where one of the gangsters is shot and killed at my father's place of business. This did happen in real life. But the interesting thing about the movie is that the man who played the policeman in that scene, actor James

McLaughlin, later became my uncle when he married my father's sister, Virginia. It just goes to show that real life is often more unusual and fascinating than anything that happens in the movies.

28

Grand Central Station

After my father's conversion, my parents' home in Los Angeles became a sort of "Grand Central Station," a busy place to which many people were drawn. Alyce Brooks was one such person. She, like my father, had committed her life to Christ at one of the Los Angeles Billy Graham meetings. Alyce had worked as a secretary for the Western Harness Racing Association at Hollywood Park. After her conversion, Alyce felt compelled to quit her job. She met my father at the Graham meetings and told him her story. She lived in a small house with her teenage daughter Virginia and she wondered how she would be able to keep up the payments now that she had no work.

My parents had a solution. They invited Alyce and Virginia to live with them. The Brooks accepted the invitation and lived with my parents, first in Baldwin Park and then in Whittier, until Mom and Dad started traveling in the trailer.

Alyce was a great help to my mother. She did babysitting and helped out around the house. And she was of spiritual encouragement to Mom. One night after my parents had given up their car, Dad phoned saying he had no way to get home–no ride and no money for the bus or streetcar. Alyce got out of bed and prayed with my mother. In about an hour my father walked into the house. A

preacher friend had driven by where Dad was waiting and brought him home.

Another person came to live with my parents from 1953 to 1954. Her name was Mickey Coy. She acted as a secretary for my father and lived with our family at 945 Edgeware Road. Dad converted the old garage into an office for Missionary Communication Service and that is where Miss Coy worked.

In 1955, Mickey Coy moved out and someone else moved in—my brother Roger was born in August of 1955. Unlike other temporary boarders, Roger lived with my parents for the next eighteen years!

The other Mickey—Cohen that is—came back into my father's life in 1956. You will remember that my father's testimony in court was instrumental in sending Cohen to jail in 1951. During the intervening years my father tried to help Mickey's wife LaVonne.

When Billy Graham had come back to Los Angeles for meetings at the Hollywood Bowl, Dad invited LaVonne to attend. She agreed to come along, so Dad drove to the once plush Brentwood home to pick her up. As my father drove up to the house he noticed the grass had died and weeds had grown up in the garden that had once been finely manicured. When a maid admitted him to the house Dad immediately recognized the carpets were gone; there was just a bare wood floor underneath his shoes. Gone too were the fine furnishings. Dad walked into the den where two years before LaVonne's friends had laughed at him for "getting religion." LaVonne looked at my father sadly and said, "The place looks a bit different, huh?"

My father couldn't help but agree.

"Remember the fun times we used to have here?"

Dad well remembered.

"Remember how the phone and the doorbell were always ringing?"

How could Dad forget? Mickey was the center of attention in Hollywood in the late 1940's.

"All the old friends are gone now. Our money is gone, so the friends are gone."

Dad and LaVonne left the empty house behind and went to pick up Sam Farkas, another of Mickey's henchmen who was now holding the fort while Mickey was in prison. The three of them went to the Hollywood Bowl and sat under the starry sky listening to a powerful message from Billy Graham. But when it came time for the invitation, neither LaVonne nor Sam made a move. Afterwards Dad introduced LaVonne to Graham. Billy spoke to her very directly about her need for Christ and she responded: "I'd be willing. I think you and Jim really have something wonderful. But I can't make the commitment unless Mickey does it with me."

Dad took LaVonne home that night. Shortly thereafter she lost the house in Brentwood. Eventually she divorced Mickey. I don't know if she ever accepted Christ as her leader and forgiver. Sam Farkas was later shot in Gardena and eventually went missing–permanently.

Mickey was doing hard time at McNeil Island Federal Penitentiary where Dad had once served out a prison sentence. But once Mickey got out of prison in 1956, Mom and Dad were there with help. How the tables were turned! My parents carried part of Mickey's rent, loaned him their Ford coupe and paid for his gas. Dad felt like Cohen had been generous to him and wanted to repay him for the way Cohen had treated him after his conversion.

What Cohen didn't tell my father was that he already had a Cadillac. He accepted Dad's car and used it, while Dad hitchhiked–long before hitchhiking became popular! Dad found out about the Cadillac from some IRS men who told him he was being played for a sucker. In turn, Dad exploded at Mickey. Cohen brought the Ford back with a lot of lame excuses attached.

In spite of incidents like that, my father remained friends with Mickey Cohen. This led some people to wonder whether my father still had connections to organized crime. He didn't. He just figured

that remaining friends with Cohen was the only way he might lead him to faith in Christ.

Dad never tried to cram religion down Mickey's throat. But Cohen would go with my father to various church meetings to hear him speak. Once, on the way back from church together, a police officer noticed Cohen in the car and stopped him.

"Where have you been today?" the officer wanted to know.

Cohen couldn't resist remarking, "We been to church!" The statement was true, but the police officer probably didn't believe a word of it.

People often ask, "Why didn't Cohen retaliate against your father for leaving the syndicate and testifying against him?" I'll let Cohen answer that question himself. He once said about my father:

"Jim's all man, but it wasn't in his make-up to get involved in violence. It was my way of life. I came up in the ranks of the syndicate because I did what I was commanded to do. I thought it was dog-eat-dog and did my job ... artistically. I never figured Jim in this category. He was kept in a certain category in my operations, different from other people. He wasn't a part of the inner circle. I never figured him to stand up in court. In fact, I told him before he went to testify, 'Look, I don't want you to lie.'

"Now, there are some others who testified against me that I really have a bad grievance against. And some got hurt for testifying against me. But Jim and some others did what they were supposed to do. If I thought they were going to do differently, I was a fool."

29

Left Behind

In the summer of 1956, the world lost a great Christian leader and Dad lost one of his best Christian friends, Dawson Trotman. Long gone were the days of tension between them. Daws gave his life saving a drowning girl at Schroon Lake, the Word of Life camp founded by evangelist Jack Wyrtzen in upstate New York. My father was present at the private funeral on the afternoon of June 27 at Glen Eyrie in Colorado. Dawson Trotman's death affected many lives, causing countless people to rededicate their few years here on earth to serving the Lord.

Dad continued his tireless trek in taking the good news of Christ through whatever open doors were provided for him. Throughout his years of travel my father logged over a million miles by land, sea and air.

In mid 1957, Dad spoke at the Christian Youth Crusade in Washington DC. After the meeting, my father went out with a group of people from the rally to a restaurant; over the meal he happened to ask if anyone present knew of a good secretary. On the way out the door, a shy young woman by the name of Betty Craig introduced herself and offered that she would like to apply for the secretarial position. Betty's home was in Glasgow, Scotland, but she was then working for the British Embassy in Washington.

Dad did some checking and found out what an excellent job Miss Craig was doing for the embassy, so he hired her the next day.

From Washington it was on to meetings at a Christian conference center on the east coast, joined by Mom, with four children in tow. Betty Craig joined our family at the conference center as well, lugging along all her worldly goods, which at that time could be contained in one trunk.

In evangelical circles in those days, smoking and drinking alcohol were certainly on the forbidden list of activities. Neither smoking nor drinking was allowed at this particular conference center. One day during our family's visit to this Christian family camp, an announcement was made in the auditorium: "Would the person who is smoking in their room please cease and desist. The fumes are spreading through the air vents and disturbing our guests." I wonder what the leaders of the conference center would have thought if they had known that the culprit was their featured speaker for the week—my father.

Unbeknownst to many outside his immediate family circle, Dad smoked cigarettes for many years, and for a brief time tried smoking a pipe. After the health hazards of smoking became more widely known in the 1960's, Dad eventually kicked the habit and never went back to it.

After the conclusion of the meetings at the Christian camp, our family, with the new addition of Betty Craig, drove to Chicago. After meetings there Dad hopped on a plane to go to another speaking engagement. No wonder my mother says that today, if she were writing a book about her life, she would entitle it: "Left Behind!" That's what my father always seemed to be doing to her: leaving her and our family behind while he was off to another engagement.

Be that as it may, Betty, Mom and kids drove from Chicago to the Navigator headquarters in Colorado where they met up with my father for one of the last board meetings of Missionary Communication Service. Today, Betty Craig describes that drive across

America as wonderful, despite a tire blowout they later experienced in Gallup, New Mexico.

Once our family arrived back in California, Betty moved in down the street from my parents at 945 Edgeware Road and took up where Mickey Coy had left off three years before. If my mother was my father's right arm, then Betty Craig quickly became his left. I don't know what Dad would have done, or what he would have become, were it not for these two women: one keeping the home fires burning, and the other keeping him organized at the office.

Betty was quickly introduced to my parents' unusual life. Soon after arriving in California she was invited to a surprise birthday party for my mother that drew a wide variety of guests, ranging from J. Lester Harnish, Pastor of Temple Baptist Church, to Mickey and LaVonne Cohen.

The following week my parents hosted another party and the renowned singer Ethel Waters was in attendance. Waters was an African American woman who had first become famous as an actress and was well known for singing the hit song: "Stormy Weather." After Waters became a Christian she said there was no more stormy weather for her; she refused to sing the song any more. She adopted a new tune as her trademark: "His Eye Is on the Sparrow." I well remember meeting Ethel Waters at the 25th Anniversary Celebration of Billy Graham's historic Los Angeles meetings. I doubt I have ever met anyone more joyful.

As mentioned in the last chapter, my parents' home in Los Angeles was becoming like Grand Central Station. They welcomed whoever came to visit, but my father grew tired of so many people inspecting his family and his lifestyle. Perhaps it reminded him too much of his childhood home; he was beginning to feel like a plastic mannequin in a store window display.

That was the trigger for my father inspecting a For Sale sign in front of a one hundred acre ranch in Grants Pass, Oregon. He was driving through the state on his way to a speaking engage-

ment in Vancouver, British Columbia. Dad enjoyed the peaceful acres he surveyed as he viewed the property. He began to dream about how relaxing it would be to come home to country serenity instead of the city thoroughfare his Los Angeles home had become. Dad phoned Mom and asked her to join him on his return trip from Vancouver.

After seeing the ranch my mother agreed to the move. My Aunt Ginny remarked to her at the time: "You'd follow that man anywhere, wouldn't you?" Mom would, and she did. The family moved to Oregon by Thanksgiving and dubbed their new home: Paradise Ranch. My father, characteristically, flew out the next day for prescheduled meetings in London, Edinburgh and Glasgow.

30

Meanwhile, Back at the Ranch

The second night at Paradise Ranch was the loneliest moment in my mother's life up to that point in time. Here she was—a girl from Hollywood—29 years old, living in a rural area, a thirty-minute drive from town and other people, with four children and no husband at home. As she later stated, she had never seen a cow face-to-face and suddenly she was running a cattle ranch.

The morning after my father left for Great Britain, Mom sent Dennis out to take the cows to pasture. My brother was eight years old and absolutely terrified. He had hardly gotten out the door when he ran back in, tears flowing and blurting out: "The cows won't let me in the gate!"

One night a state trooper came by to inform my mother that her cattle were out on the road. She wondered, "My cattle?" At that point she was probably ready to pack up and head back to California, wondering what on earth she was doing on a ranch in Oregon. But she plodded on with God's help.

Meanwhile, Dad was traveling and speaking in the British Isles, following up meetings Billy Graham had held in 1954 and 1955. My father had been in Scotland in 1956 and heard an incredible singing group called the "Festival of Male Voice Praise." There were one hundred voices in the all male choir, many of them coal

miners and the like. Dad had never heard such singing anywhere. The rolling of their R's, the trilling of their T's and the simplicity of their style stayed in my father's mind and heart for a long time. Most of all, it was the manner in which this group of men honored Jesus Christ; that was what most impressed Dad. This choral group spent as much time in prayer as they spent in performance.

In his mind, Dad began to scheme how he could bring this music to America. Recording in those days involved a complicated use of acetate; then there was wire recording and finally tape recording.

As mentioned earlier, Dad used a lot of electronic equipment in his high school, college and church presentations during the 1950's. One of the best pieces of equipment that he had at that time was a recorder manufactured by Ampex in Redwood City, California. The men at Ampex liked the free publicity so they agreed to let my father demonstrate a new product: stereophonic recording equipment. The machine they gave Dad was among the first pieces of stereo equipment, almost unheard of at that time. They promised to have a finished unit packed in steamer luggage for Dad's use in the near future.

As soon as my father had the finished product in hand, he was eager to make recordings. However, he was blocked by the musician's union. The military was more helpful. They allowed Dad to record the Air Force Symphony Orchestra, then the Navy Band, both in Washington DC. In Freeport, Illinois, my father recorded one of the last of the big steam powered railroad engines. He recorded it in such a way that when played back in a large auditorium with the lights out, it was a frightening experience. It rattled the timbers in Kleinhans Music Hall in Buffalo, New York. The whistle blew in the middle of the auditorium and the sound of the lengthy train moved across the audience, finally fading into the night.

All of this realism in sound brought back memories of the unforgettable Scotsmen. Recording them was far more complicated

than recording bands, symphonies or even trains. But thanks to the BBC in London, Dad soon learned what it would take to record the Scotsmen. That is, beside his hundred-pound, three-channel, ½ inch stereophonic recorder.

He learned that he would have to convert from fifty-cycle to sixty-cycle, and from 220 to 110 volts, to say nothing of transportation via New York to Glasgow. But with the wonderful help of director James McRoberts of the "Festival of Male Voice Praise," Dad pulled it off. Arrangements were made to record in St. George's Cross Tabernacle (now known as Findlay Memorial Church) in the heart of Glasgow in December 1957.

My father returned home in time for Christmas. Betty Craig moved from Los Angeles to Paradise Ranch after spending Christmas at her home in Scotland. Back in the United States, she loaded a one hundred foot radio tower plus all of Dad's office equipment in and on top of a station wagon. As a novice driver, making her way over the Siskiyou Mountains, in the winter snow on a two lane road with tractor-trailer trucks bearing down on her, was terrifying. But Betty was a real "trooper" so she didn't let her nervousness get the better of her.

The children in our family—even though they were "city kids"—made a rapid adjustment to rural life on the ranch. One favorite activity was racing across the middle of the cow pen, until the cows were nerved by it and threw their weight around. And then there was the day my siblings failed to take into account the previous day of rain and its effect on the layer of manure covering the ground. The rain transformed the future fertilizer into quick sand. Any movement they made to pull themselves out of the cow dung only served to get them more surely rooted in the muck.

Paradise Ranch is where my brother Steve started to play the guitar and began dreaming of being a rock and roll star someday. In fact, he is in the music industry today, working as a singer, songwriter and producer. He has had his own radio program and is beginning

to branch out into television. Steve has many happy memories of Oregon—of Dad teaching him to ride a bike on the gravel driveway behind the farmhouse, the old swayback horse Pokey, ducks gliding across the pond, the first snowfall and making a snowman.

However, Grants Pass is also the place where my brother Roger had a calamity that he almost didn't survive. Six-year-old Steve was sailing a toy boat on the pond in front of the house. Along came three-year-old Roger and when the boat sailed past him, he reached out to grab it. Unfortunately the boat was just beyond his reach. Before Steve knew it, Roger, who did not know how to swim, had fallen in the pond. Steve ran to get Mom. When she pulled Roger out of the water he was blue. Panic set in. She brought him back to the house and telephoned for an ambulance. As my mother laid her youngest child on the kitchen floor all she could think of was the hymn, "O Love That Will Not Let Me Go." And she must have prayed: "Lord, don't let him go." The Lord didn't let Roger go—the local ambulance squad arrived soon enough, went into action, and my brother survived.

Roger's calamity was followed by another family tragedy. My sister Alissa was born in September 1959 and from the beginning of her life had endless problems. She had a convulsion when she was a few weeks old. The doctor at the hospital didn't know the cause, but Alissa was bleeding internally, in her head. In time she seemed to recover and the doctor sent her home. But the problems only intensified. Mom took Alissa to the University of Oregon hospital in Portland for treatment. The staff explained her problem: fluid was building up in Alissa's head. Mom got her hands on a medical book and looked up Alissa's condition: hydrocephalus, water on the brain. Today this problem can be cured, but in 1959 it mystified the medical profession.

Alissa was taken to Portland for seven operations, with the family hoping against hope, but the operations did not help. Eventu-

ally Alissa lost her sight, then her hearing. Heartbreakingly, my family could no longer keep Alissa at home; she was too sick. Her many physical needs necessitated her receiving care in a pediatric nursing home. My mother laid Alissa in another's arms, somehow knowing she was not to have her little girl again here on earth.

Up to that point my family had desperately prayed, asking the Lord to heal Alissa. But after the many fruitless operations Mom remembers kneeling at the side of Alissa's empty crib at home praying that most difficult prayer: "Not our will but Thine be done." As my mother later put it in a booklet she wrote about the whole ordeal, eventually "our 'littlest angel' went home to be with God. Our precious jewel is forever safe with Him who loved us so much that He gave His son!"[7]

The loss of Alissa was a reminder to my parents that finding a full life in Christ does not exempt one from problems, heartache, illness and even death. But in the midst of the emptiness Alissa left behind, my parents discovered a peace that passes understanding. It was to take some time for our family to recover from this loss. But in the meantime the Lord had new plans for my father, and for our family, to give us hope and a future.

Grandpa Jim:
James Arthur Vaus, Sr

Grandma Lillie:
Lillie Meyer Vaus

1920 | *Dad as a child*

1936 | *Belmont Knights (Dad is in the back row, 4th from the left)*

1938 | *On a mission in Canada, age 19*

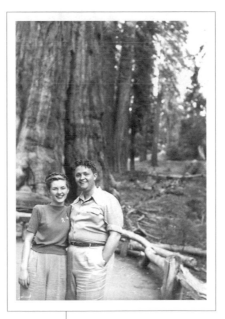

c. 1946 | *Mom and Dad on a date in the Redwoods*

1947 | October 23:
Mom and Dad's wedding day

c. 1949 | Dad with Mickey Cohen
during his gangster days.

1949 | *In the Canvas Cathedral (From left: Cliff Barrows, Harvey Fritts, Dad, Stuart Hamblen, Louis Zamperini, Billy Graham)*

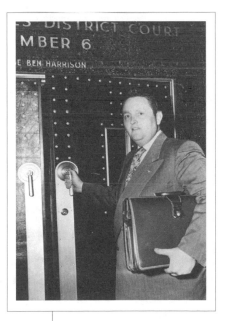

1951 | *Dad was subpoenaed to testify against Mickey Cohen*

1951 | *Dad showing Mickey Cohen his book,*
Why I Quit Syndicated Crime

1955 | *Dad spoke to a large CBMC group in Detroit (Dad is front and center)*

1955 | A Wiretapper *movie poster*

c. 1955 | *Dad with Tesla Coil*

1956 | *Family (Youngest to oldest: Roger, Steve, Dennis, Madeline, Mom, Dad)*

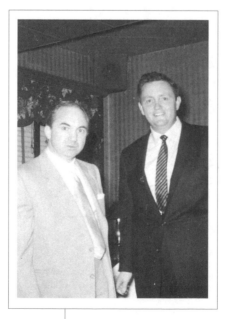

c. 1957 | *Dad and Cohen after Cohen was released from prison*

c. 1957 | *Dad talking to inquirers in England*

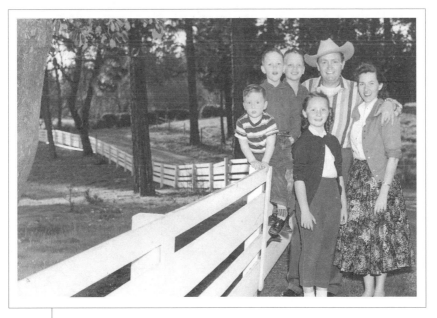

1958 | *Family in Oregon*

1960 | *Billy Graham with Dad*

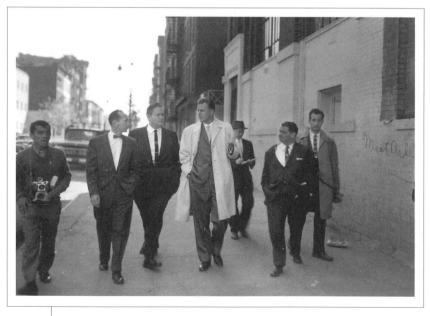

1960 | *Dad and Billy on the streets of East Harlem*

1960 | *Dad and Billy while Billy was visiting NYC (Billy is holding a homemade gun from Harlem)*

c. 1960 | *Dad at 2110 Second Avenue, NYC*

c. 1960 | *Dad in front of the post office, Hell Gate Station, NYC*

c. 1960 | *Dad with his electronic gear*

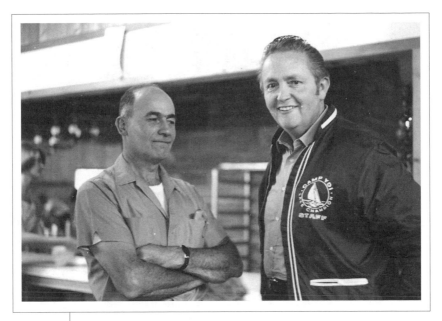

c. 1967 | *Dad and Miller Fagley*

1968 | *Me, Mom, Mark Hatfield, his son Mark O., and Dad, at*
Camp Champion

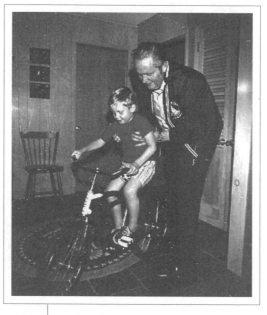

1968 | *Dad helping me on the bike*
(Photo by Russ Busby)

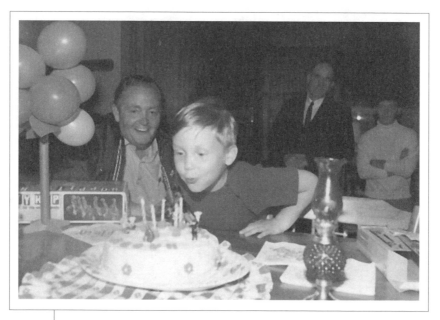

1968 | *My birthday (Photo by Russ Busby)*

1968 | *Family at Camp Champion (Youngest to oldest: Will, Roger, Steve, Dennis, Mom, Dad)*

c. 1968 | *Dad in the Tarrytown office with computer equipment*

c. 1968 | *Dad with Harlem boys at Camp Champion*

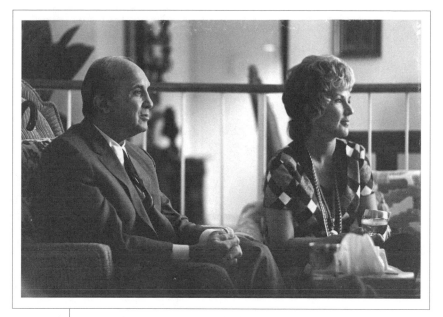

c. 1973 | *Mom and Mickey Cohen in his apartment in Westwood, CA*
(Photo by Russ Busby)

1974 | *Dad and me in front of Big Ben*

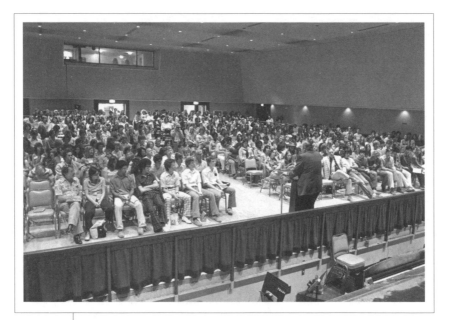

c. 1975 | *Dad speaking to San Diego honor students at the old San Diego Convention Center*

c. 1975 | *Dad teaching electronics in our garage to boys from Sam's Ranch*

1979 | Dad with his two sisters, Betty
Rothenberger and Virginia
McLaughlin

1979 | Mom and Dad

1983 | *Steve, Dad, me and Mom with Billy Graham at his Sacramento, CA crusade (Photo by Russ Busby)*

1984 | *Dad and Billy at the 35th anniversary of the 1949 Los Angeles meetings, when a commemorative plaque was installed near the corner of Washington & Hill (Photo by Russ Busby)*

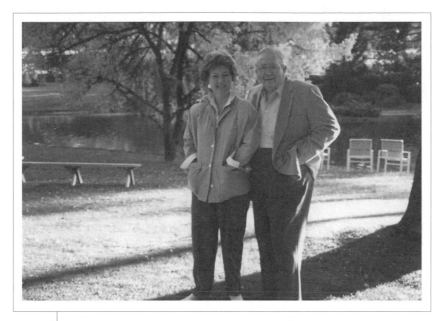

1986 | *Mom and Dad, revisiting Paradise Ranch, Oregon*

1987 | *Dad and sons*

1988 | Dad with Dave and Darlene Swanson, two of the original YDI board members

1989 | Mom and Dad with Billy in Beverly Hills when he had his star placed on Hollywood Blvd. (Photo by Russ Busby)

c. 1990 | *YDI staff with Mike MacIntosh*

1992 | *Family at my ordination (From left: Uncle Jim, Aunt Ginny, Corrie, Steve, Mom, Dad, me, Becky, Dennis, Lorrie, Roger)*

1993 | *Me, my son James, and Dad, on the occasion of my son's baptism*

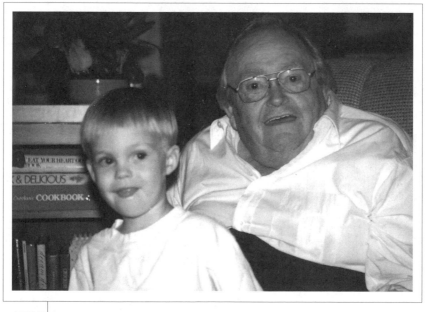

1995 | *My son James and Dad in Head Waters, VA*

1994 | *Family gathering for Dad's 75th birthday, on February 17*
(Counter-clockwise from left: Steve and his wife Corrie, Steve's daughters
Emily and Amanda, Roger and his wife Lorrie, Becky holding our son
James, me, Dennis and his wife Kathie, Mom, Dad in the middle)

PART THREE:

Filling Other's Emptiness

(1958-1970)

31

A Heart for Juvenile Delinquents

Whenever I would travel with my father to one of his speaking engagements, he would invariably introduce me as his "personal juvenile delinquent." All kidding aside, Dad always had an interest in helping youthful offenders because he could identify with their problems. In 1953, he published another book, again with the help of Dorothy Haskin. This one was entitled *The Inside Story of Narcotics*, and in 1956 there was a third book, *Teenage Rampage*. Dad little knew at that point exactly how much he was going to have to deal with teen rampage and teen drug problems over the course of the rest of his life.

In Oregon my father got to know the Secretary of State, Mark Hatfield. Hatfield later became Governor of Oregon and then a United States Senator. Dad admired Hatfield as a young Christian politician.

Dad was invited to tour a state prison, along with one of Hatfield's associates. The idea of going back into jail sent chills up and down my father's spine. But this experience was different from his previous incarceration; as a guest of Mark Hatfield he was given royal treatment. As Dad went through the receiving line, greeting all of the staff, there was one man who needed no introduction. It was Warden Spires whom Dad had known at McNeil Island Fed-

eral Penitentiary. Dad liked him a lot better when he wasn't looking at him through iron bars!

That prison visit was the start of a whole lot of thinking my father did about how he could help juvenile delinquents. Dad's own church had shunned him when he first got into trouble, right at the time he most needed guidance. My father wanted to make sure that other youth did not feel ostracized from the church; he wanted them to see Christians reaching out in love.

Subsequently, my father took every opportunity that came his way to speak to young people, especially those behind bars. Many had been incarcerated for years as punishment for horrific crimes. Dad would tell his story about how Jesus had changed his life. Kids listened because he shared something in common with them: a juvenile prison record.

On one of my father's speaking tours he found himself at the Eastern State Penitentiary in Pennsylvania. After what he thought had been a provocative talk, a sixteen year old young man, who was serving out a life sentence for killing a police officer, approached my father and said: "Mr. Vaus, it was a good talk you gave today. But it would have been better if you had reached us before we got here." The words of that young man reverberated in my father's mind for some time.

Dad's next stop after the penitentiary was New York City where he spoke at a series of meetings for church-going young people sponsored by Percy Crawford. They were good kids and Dad could see they were getting something out of his messages, but he couldn't stop thinking about what the sixteen year old at Eastern State had said. At the close of Crawford's meetings, my father took a walking tour of Manhattan on a cool April evening in 1958.

He started at Greenwich Village and worked his way up to Fifty-Seventh Street. Dad stopped at a newsstand and bought a copy of *Life* magazine. There was an article in *Life* about the trouble several gangs were causing in NYC. Dad stood on the street corner

devouring every word of that article. It was frightening. The young people it talked about were poor African Americans or Puerto Ricans to whom no one was paying any attention except for the trouble they were stirring up. These youth were staging all-out wars on the city streets and sometimes completely innocent people were getting hurt as well. Furthermore, the problem was growing. (Interestingly enough, around the same time, the Lord was working on another one of his servants, inspiring him to move from Pennsylvania to minister to the troubled youth of New York. David Wilkerson eventually started Teen Challenge and wrote *The Cross and the Switchblade* about his experience.)

My father looked up from his magazine and saw beautiful people in fur coats; they looked as though they had just stepped out of Bergdorf Goodman's. As Dad walked and watched people he couldn't help but think of the contrast between these chic city slickers and the kids on the other side of town who were condemned to a life deprived of physical, emotional and spiritual nourishment. Couldn't something be done to meet the needs of these "throwaway" young people? Dad sensed God calling him to do something to help.

32

Surveying the Problem

My father was in New York for a few more days so he decided to go to the New York Public Library and do some research on gang violence in the city. He learned there were fourteen areas in the five boroughs listed as particularly high in crime. At the top of the list was the 23rd Precinct in Spanish Harlem, that part of East Harlem running from 96th to 119th Streets, the East River to Central Park. This one square mile had the densest population, 196,000 people, and the highest crime rate of any one square mile in the world at that time. In this one small area there were forty-nine different street gangs, populated by five thousand hostile, unloved and undisciplined teenagers. The police department had four hundred foot patrolmen on the beat and was spending a half-million dollars each month to curb crime, just in this one area.

My father took the subway uptown in order to gather his own impressions. The streets were far different from his midtown starting point. The sidewalks looked and smelled as though the garbage truck had dumped its excess refuse on them. Dad heard whistles go off down the street like an alarm. It was all because of him. The kids must have thought he was a police officer. As he passed the post office he couldn't help but notice it was called Hell Gate Station, a name taken from the geographical area. Years before, residents had

noticed that where the Harlem and East Rivers came together there was a tempestuous spot. They called it the Devil's Boiling Pot, or the Gate of Hell. Thus the adjacent land came to be known as Hell Gate. Dad thought the name must well describe the way it would feel to live in the area. This teeming square mile held out its invitation to my father: Try if you dare to tackle the problems here.

The next night Dad spoke at a Times Square church and mentioned his concern for the youth of Harlem. Afterwards an elderly woman came up and slipped a piece of paper into his hand saying, "Here's the name of a man you should get in touch with." The name on the paper was Conrad S. Jensen, police captain in the 23rd Precinct.

Dad phoned Jensen and told him about the lady who had given him the piece of paper. "That was my mother," Jensen replied. Dad asked for an appointment, which was quickly set up for the following Monday morning.

My father called home and told my mother he would be delayed in getting back to Oregon. The next Monday, as scheduled, Dad met with Captain Jensen. My father told the policeman he was thinking of moving to East Harlem to try to help with the gang problem and put kids in touch with Christ. My father noticed a Bible on Jensen's desk, as he heard the captain reply: "I've been praying for God to send a man like you to our streets."

Conrad Jensen went on to explain to my father what life was like on the streets of Spanish Harlem: nine year old children hustling to survive, boys becoming fathers by the age of fourteen. The raw energy of 196,000 people rubbing shoulders in such a small space would often ignite violence. Kids from fourteen and up would develop elaborate gang structures. They might carry anything as a weapon: zip guns made out of wood, rubber bands and pipe. Some had real guns.

Dad wanted to get inside the minds of these troubled youth and offer them something more than the life they were seeing on

the streets. The first step was to provide a safe place where the kids could get off the streets. My father asked Jensen if he had any suggestions for a place to establish a club, a place he could live in as well. The captain knew of an empty storefront. It had been a florist shop and now was very run down. Dad rented it immediately.

Captain Jensen recommended a contractor to do the renovations: Arnold Thompson. Dad and Thompson did a walk-through together; as they meandered through the rat and lice-infested building they risked their legs going through decayed floorboards with every step. My father described to the contractor what he wanted the place to look like. A wall would need to be knocked out, windows inviting break-in would need to be boarded up; the glass door would need to be replaced. Dad concluded all they could really use was the address: 2110 Second Avenue. Thompson took on the challenge of turning a dump in the middle of a concrete desert into something attractive to youth.

Dad figured he had only a few other arrangements to make. He would need money, and he would need to explain to my mom what he had in mind. En route to Oregon he stopped at the Billy Graham Evangelistic Association offices in Minneapolis. He told Mr. Graham's team what he had in mind to do in New York. They made their office available for Dad to use to prepare his first fund-raising mailing. He wrote to everyone he had come in contact with through almost ten years of traveling around the world as an evangelist, and shared his vision.

Once Dad reached Grants Pass he told Mom of his plans. She had already been through so much with my father that nothing took her by surprise. As she listened to my father describe his vision for reaching the youth in Spanish Harlem, she became his first, most important and ardent supporter, despite the fact that it would mean another temporary separation for my parents.

Dad stayed a few extra days in Grants Pass because he knew his next separation from his family would be a longer one. He made

sure Mom had enough money and that extra hands were hired to work the ranch. My father loaded all of his electronic equipment on to a two and a half ton truck and left early on a Sunday morning to make a speaking engagement at the First Baptist Church of Grants Pass. What Mom didn't know was that he had left her all the money he had in the world. He didn't even take out enough money for himself to purchase gas to get to New York, let alone to buy meals along the way.

That morning in church, Dad openly shared with the congregation how the words of the downhearted boy he had met in Eastern State Penitentiary had such a dramatic impact on him and had inspired his vision to reach out to kids in Spanish Harlem before they reached prison. He described the storefront he had rented and the club for boys he hoped to start. Before driving off, a man from the congregation came up and pressed $50 into Dad's hand and a credit card to pay the necessary expenses for my father to get to New York. The first hurdle in Dad's next race was overcome.

33

The House on Second Avenue

When Dad drove up to 2110 Second Avenue in the late spring of 1958, Arnold Thompson had done his work. The windows were blacked out and a wall was built inside of them. There was a strong wooden door in place of the old glass one. Inside, the place was transformed into a clubhouse. There was a new floor, paint and paneling. There was a bed in the back for Dad to sleep in, and a special counseling room in the front. In between, there was a room where Dad could teach about electronics, plus a snack bar. In order to tighten security, my father rigged up a closed circuit television inside with a camera outside, and an intercom system so he could see and talk to anyone at the door before letting them in.

My father received a detailed description of the local gang structure from Connie Jensen, including names and addresses of gang leaders. Dad tried finding each one of them to personally invite them to his club, but they were nowhere to be found. He would climb the steps of one tenement building only to be told: "No one here by that name," or "Try the next building over." He would get to the next building only to be told the young man in question didn't live there either. That was the story everywhere Dad went in East Harlem.

Apparently a false report had gotten around that Dad was a cop. Other rumors floated too: "He's a government official investigating the boys of East Harlem." or "He's a member of the New York Crime Commission," or "He's a leader of the Communist Party!"

As time passed, Dad got more and more lonely. Thompson would drop in every now and again with donuts and coffee and conversation. Or my father would stop by to see Connie Jensen, but he was often quite busy with his police work. The days were as hot as the name on the front of the post office that summer in Hell Gate. The garbage on the streets started to stink more than usual. Dad later said that his idle time in those first few months in Spanish Harlem were worse than his time in prison.

Meanwhile he continued to have countless invitations pour in to speak all over the country. Many Christians said he was foolish to turn down the opportunity to speak to thousands just to reach a few forgotten kids in Manhattan. What they didn't know was that Dad wasn't even able to reach those youth—not at first. My father was like the shepherd in Jesus' story, leaving the ninety-nine sheep on the hillside to go and look for the one that was lost. Only he hadn't yet found that one lost sheep.

My father was encouraged during this time by the words of a song he helped to record. The words were written by Margaret Clarkson and the music by John W. Peterson:

So send I you to labor unrewarded,
To serve unpaid, unloved, unsought, unknown,
To bear rebuke, to suffer scorn and scoffing–
So send I you to toil for Me alone.[8]

By September the air turned cooler in New York and Dad was looking to Jefferson Park Junior High School, with its two thousand students, as his last shot to reach the kids of Harlem. With a

good word from Captain Jensen, my father approached Ed Gersh, the dean of discipline at the school and asked him for his help. Gersh asked him whom he represented.

Dad said, "No one."

"Well, for whom do you work?"

Dad again said, "No one."

"And who finances this?"

"No one."

"Well, on what approved list do you appear for the State of New York or the City of New York?"

"None."

"Well I can't see ..." said Gersh as he got up to leave.

Stopping him, Dad said: "Wait a minute. I'm not looking for a place to live. I have a home out west. Let me tell you why I've come." My father went on to tell Ed Gersh how he had come to know Christ.

Gersh replied, very uncomfortably: "Well, come and see me in school tomorrow."

The following day Dad went to the school. Gersh ushered him out of his office and into that of the school psychiatrist! From there it was on to see the principal, Israel Flax. Dad talked about the electronics show, his clubhouse, and his plans for trying to help the kids of East Harlem to build better relationships with each other. When my father left, Gersh said to Flax: "What do you think boss?" Flax responded, "I think Vaus may be a help, Eddie."

Flax and Gersh met with my father again and gave him a double dose of the training they usually gave to new teachers at Jefferson Park, fully preparing him for the language, the behavior and the hopelessness of these young people. A week later, Dad showed up at the school with his truckload of electronics. My father unloaded thousands of pounds of equipment without any help and then set everything up on the school auditorium stage. Gersh and Flax were impressed. They were even more impressed by the show. So were

the kids. The students began watching with "show me" expressions on their faces. In the end, they loved it.

Dad gave them a full-dress performance. He jolted the students out of their apathy with five-foot high speakers playing marches in stereo–something the kids had never heard before. The recording of the railroad was a smash hit–it sounded like it was splitting the auditorium in half. My father also let the audience listen to millions of molecules in a piece of steel.

Dad recruited volunteers and projected their voices off beams of light. He pumped almost a million volts through a boy's body and let him light a fluorescent bulb with his fingertips. As with all his audiences, my father showed the students the hidden colors of God's creation brought out by black light.

By October, kids were swarming around the house on Second Avenue. Kids started bringing their friends to the clubhouse. There was such a crowd in the small storefront that Dad had to issue membership cards. Youth Development, Inc. (YDI) was born.

34

Youth Development, Inc.

One of the first young gang leaders to whom my father was introduced was Eddie Suarez, war counselor for the Dragons. Eddie had been shot twice in the abdomen in a gang war. Dad had the chance to befriend Eddie after his recovery and was able to help the young man with a number of personal problems. Many months later, in their discussions about God, the Bible and Jesus Christ, Eddie realized that God had a perfect plan for his life. So it was, in the house on Second Avenue, that Eddie knelt and committed his life to Jesus Christ. He was the first gang leader to do so during Dad's ministry in New York.

Amazingly, Dad told Eddie, "Don't tell anyone about your decision. Take this Bible. Read it, study it; meditate upon it." My father also passed on to Eddie the Navigator's Topical Memory System he himself had used to memorize Scripture. Dad again stressed that Eddie should not yet tell anyone about his newfound relationship with Jesus Christ, not even his mother. Rather, Dad urged, "As you permit God to transform your life, and as you follow him with dedication, the change will become apparent to all."

One evening, about midnight, Dad was walking along Second Avenue with now Inspector Jensen. A social worker stopped

them saying, "Vaus, have you had any contact with this guy named Suarez?"

Dad said, "Yes, I know him."

The social worker continued, "Have you noticed the change in his life lately?"

My father countered, "What do you mean?"

The social worker went on to mention some of the changes in Eddie that were apparent to him. Later my father said, "Why not talk to Eddie? Ask him what happened." By this time Eddie was busting at the seams to share his newfound faith.

After that, many people noticed the change in Suarez. Eddie went on to serve two years with the armed forces in Germany. He returned to New York, got married and had a child. He then served as an indigenous leader with YDI.

In the autumn of 1977, Dad met up again with Eddie Suarez, after a separation of a number of years. Suarez had become an important part of the New York City government and an outstanding civic leader in Hell Gate. Each of his family members had become Christians. His daughter, grown up by that time, had gone on to study at Harvard University.

Returning to 1959—the mailings my father was sending out about his work in New York were bringing in about one thousand dollars per month. It was time to form a board of directors for this fledgling ministry. Many of the men Dad recruited for the board were men he had met through Connie Jensen and the Christian Business Mens' Committee. The first man Dad asked to be on the board was Arnold Thompson, the contractor who had renovated 2110. Next, my father asked George "Gus" Lambrides, a certified public accountant, to act as treasurer, handling all the money and writing the checks. A separate accounting firm audited the accounts starting from day one. Attorney Julius B. Poppinga was the architect of Youth Development's corporate structure and bylaws. Pop-

pinga applied to the IRS for Youth Development to be recognized as a nonprofit corporation. Dave Swanson, one of the owner's of S. B. Thomas, Inc., creator of Thomas' English Muffins, along with his wife, Darlene, also joined the board, along with Alex Sampson. In the beginning, my father sat on the board of YDI. But after a time, deeming his board position and his status as paid employee to be a conflict of interest, Dad became Executive Director.

Youth Development, Inc. was incorporated June 17, 1959. YDI was, from the beginning, a privately funded, nonprofit, nondenominational, nonpolitical corporation. Its mission was the promotion of "the physical, social, cultural and spiritual welfare of urban youth, the development of a vital godliness and a moral conscience among them, and the establishment and maintenance of a witness, to urban youth and others, for the Gospel of Jesus Christ as revealed in the Holy Scriptures."[9]

A Sunday school class was needed to disciple the many teens making commitments to Christ just as Eddie Suarez had. Dad checked around for a church that would open its doors to his gang kids. Calvary Baptist Church on West 57th Street invited the YDI kids to join their teen Sunday school class. Bright and early on a September Sunday morning, Dad went pounding on apartment doors, on car windows, and in alleys. The kids wanted to go to Sunday school but it was up to Dad to get them to church on time. When Dad had gathered all the interested teens, the group of nine journeyed to midtown Manhattan in Dad's station wagon. It was truly an adventure for these kids who had never ventured as far as 57th Street.

Joining in the regular Sunday school class didn't work for long. That was before the days of civil rights; when churchgoers got a look at the YDI crowd, many of their noses were in the air. The church soon found Dad a room of his own where he could teach his own class.

Numbers grew. The station wagon was replaced with a bus, then two. Dad ended up with a hundred kids, all types, from gang leaders to girls with babies, all coming to Sunday school. The church, apparently embarrassed, or perhaps just overrun, finally asked Dad to use Steinway Hall, a building down the street, at the church's expense.

One of the first staffers who joined YDI in those early days was John (Petey) Thomas, who dropped by the police precinct one day in 1959 while Dad was talking to Connie Jensen. Thomas was fresh out of Sing Sing Correctional Facility where he had served a sentence for armed robbery and felonious assault. Thomas managed to get a job as a foreman in a bakery and he was determined to clean up his life. My father would often stop by the bakery to try to recruit Thomas to work for YDI. Eventually, he accepted Dad's invitation.

Petey knew Harlem and he also spoke the language of the streets. He started out talking to kids at the local hangout–the candy store. Because of where he had been, teens listened to Thomas, and he listened to them.

Dad and Thomas both realized the two things kids in Harlem were missing: discipline and love. My father was not ashamed to put his arm around the shoulder of a boy and let him know somebody cared. But both he and Thomas could talk and act tough when they needed to. And to the shock of some, Dad was not averse to hitting back when things got violent.

Some Christians said, "Shouldn't you turn the other cheek?" Dad countered with one of his favorite Bible verses, "Whatsoever thy hand findeth to do, do it with thy might" (Ecclesiastes 9:10). By standing tough, Dad earned respect among the youth of Harlem. Many came back years later and thanked him for providing a discipline they had never known before.

When there was no other way to settle a gang dispute, YDI staffers would let the two gang leaders duke it out. Other social service agencies looked askance at YDI's methods. But those methods worked–most of the time.

35

The Good Lopez Boy

One evening at twilight my father drove up to his storefront with
a carload of boys. Santos Lopez and his brother Goldie were wait-
ing outside. "Mr. Jim, can we talk?" Santy called over the noise of
the boys piling out of the station wagon. Santy and Goldie got in
and Dad drove off.

Fifteen-year-old Santy had become a Christian when Dad took
him and some other boys to Pinebrook Bible Conference Center
in July 1959. When Santy came back from camp, others recognized
there was something different about him. He was known as "the
boy with the smile" or "the good Lopez boy" because he was the
only one among his brothers who wasn't involved in gangs. Santy
Lopez was voted "Most Likely to Succeed" at Public School 117.

When Santy hopped into Dad's station wagon he explained
that a gang on 109th Street was after his brother Goldie. They
were planning to "burn" him for holding out on drugs. "But he
doesn't have any," Santy pleaded. The boys fed my father the rest
of the details they had about the planned shooting. Dad said he
would do his best to "cool it" then he dropped the Lopez boys at
their apartment.

My father went to dinner, planning in his mind some strategy
for how to stop this "bopping." On his way back to 2110 he received

a call on his car telephone. Santy was dead, shot in the back. Dad rushed to 117th and 3rd Avenue and found Santy's blood still fresh on the sidewalk. He made his way to the Lopez apartment. As he entered, Santy's mother embraced him. A photographer from the New York Post snapped their photo and the story was in the paper the next day, May 26, 1960. Blazoned on the front page was the headline: SLAY WRONG BOY IN TEEN WAR. As if there could be a right boy. From behind, Santy had been mistaken for Goldie.

Dad spoke at Santy's funeral. "From the day Santos became a Christian his Bible was his proud possession, and his life a living testimony. He was president of the Sunday school class–faithful, even if it meant walking many blocks in the rain."

The Sunday after the funeral, six members of the Lopez family came to Sunday school. At the end of the meeting, all six accepted Christ. "We want what Santy had." And Goldie said, "I want to take Santy's place. I will live for Christ no matter what the other kids say."

Boys weren't the only ones getting into trouble in East Harlem. Girls got into gang fights every bit as nasty as the guys. Dad didn't have room for any more people at 2110 so he was considering opening a separate club for girls when he met Mrs. Lyn Robinson at New Hyde Park Baptist Church where he was speaking one day. Lyn cared about the problems of girls in Hell Gate and volunteered to help. In 1959, YDI opened a storefront operation for girls on 108th Street. The main attraction was the beauty shop.

The volunteers who helped were wonderful, but they were not trained to handle hard-core gang girls. So Dad hired Vete Rust, a young woman who had done great work with girls' gangs in Chicago. If the girls got out of hand, Vete was not afraid to rush into the middle of a fight. She would help when girls got pregnant or had trouble in court; she would lend a hand any way she could.

When Dad first went to Harlem, he thought he might spend a few months there and then hand on the work to others. But

when it became apparent he was needed in New York long-term, he decided it was time for our family to move. Mom came from Oregon and spent a week with Dad at 2110. They looked for a house and found the perfect place in Tarrytown, north of NYC on the Hudson River. There was a house being built in a neighborhood atop the hill in Tarrytown, overlooking the Tappan Zee Bridge. It was close enough for Dad to commute to work in the city. The six-bedroom house was built at 17 Heritage Court and our family moved from west coast to east in the summer of 1960.

A Different Kind of Notoriety

My father had been mentioned in newspapers and national magazines many times because of his involvement in organized crime. So in the early 60's, it was a new thing for Dad to be recognized nationally as a gang-buster instead of a gangster. From the very start the news media took interest in what my father was doing in East Harlem. In the summer of 1959, there was a front page story in the New York Herald Tribune.

Dad also began to meet the movers and shakers of New York. Dad's friend, Oregon Governor Mark Hatfield, came to visit him at 2110 on November 17, 1959. Hatfield introduced my father to the Governor of New York, Nelson A. Rockefeller, in a meeting at Rockefeller's home outside of Tarrytown. Humorously enough, Rockefeller had never met Hatfield, and so when the two men walked up to him at his mansion, Rockefeller extended his hand to my father first and said, "Welcome Governor Hatfield!" Subsequent to that meeting Rockefeller arranged for my father to serve as a consultant to the State of New York's Task Force on Youth and Juvenile Delinquency.

Mark Hatfield also arranged for Dad to meet and have an extended conversation with former President Herbert Hoover. One of the many framed photos of famous people my father had in his

office for a number of years was of President Hoover. The President signed the photo, "To James Vaus, The Good Wishes of Herbert Hoover." By February 1961, Dad's work in Spanish Harlem had even drawn the attention of President Kennedy.

In the autumn of 1960, another famous face came through the door of 2110 Second Avenue–Billy Graham. Dad had invited Graham to speak to seventy influential leaders from forty-nine gangs in Hell Gate. Despite his incredibly busy schedule, Graham accepted the invitation. When he came to Harlem and walked the streets with the teens, visiting their families, he really made an impact. Mr. Graham spoke to the kids at 2110, giving them a straight gospel presentation. Dad concluded with the story of his own conversion. Many had never heard the story before; tears ran down some cheeks. When Graham gave the invitation over half of the teens present raised their hands to accept Christ.

Graham's YDI fan club was already strong when he visited in October 1960 because his wife Ruth had given to the club a soda fountain she and Billy had received when he was a guest on the TV show, *This Is Your Life*. Dad had just the right place for that soda fountain. He put it in the snack bar at 2110 where the Coke machine used to be. My father learned early on that the Coke machine just wasn't going to work in his club. When the distributor came to collect the proceeds the first time, there was no money—and no Coke left! The soda fountain worked much better and the boys came up with some of the wildest ice cream concoctions known to humanity.

By this time Dad and the staff of eight he had working with him were reaching half of the forty-nine gangs in the square mile of Hell Gate. In 1960, juvenile crime in New York City had climbed by 8.9%, but in Youth Development's square mile it had dropped by 19.5%, even by 30% in the heart of that square mile. This drew the attention of newspapers and national magazines.

On December 19, 1960 an article in Time magazine reported: *As the moving spirits of a remarkably successful East Harlem rehabilitation mission named Youth Development Inc., Vaus and Thomas are two of the most expert bop-busters in the business.*[10]

Time was referring to Dad and Thomas' gift for settling gang disputes, a gift which was often exercised in the basement of our home in Tarrytown. Dad felt the key was to get gang leaders off the streets, out of the city and on to neutral turf. Thus he would bring them, in our Ford station wagon, up the New York State Thruway and out to the suburbs, where he became a peacemaker in our own home.

In June 1961 Ebony had a six page article on YDI. The article began:

In the tough, deprived slum jungle that is East Harlem, two ex-convicts, armed only with love and faith and aided by a tiny band of dedicated volunteers, are successfully waging a small war against juvenile crime. Both men, Jim Vaus and John (Petey) Thomas, once knew crime from the inside and served prison terms before deep spiritual changes led them to devote their time to keeping hundreds of lost and vagrant youths out of trouble.[11]

In July 1961, Reader's Digest ran a feature article entitled: "The Two Lives of Jim Vaus." In that article, Robert P. Crossley wrote,

In the vortex of violence and hatred that is Spanish Harlem, New York's toughest district, Jim Vaus, a husky 285 pounds, moves quietly among 40 or more gangs. Time and again he heads off "boppings" (gang fights) and dissuades young toughs from crimes that might send them to prison for life. He is the founder of a unique organization called Youth Development, Inc, which operates from behind a boarded-up storefront on Second Avenue. Yet

he is far from the popular conception of a "youth worker." He has been in plenty of trouble himself. The toughest kid in Harlem knows that Jim Vaus speaks from experience because he has been "on the other side."[12]

All the publicity in national magazines led to a Time-Life film team getting interested in the work of YDI. They produced "Petey and Johnny", a documentary film about YDI with Petey Thomas as their star. It was later released on NBC TV. Petey, who had wanted to try his hand at writing, eventually left YDI. He devoted his time to writing a book about Spanish Harlem which became a nation-wide bestseller entitled, *Down These Mean Streets*.

37

Changed Lives

Petey Thomas, Eddie Suarez and Santy Lopez weren't the only lives touched and changed by YDI. They were just the first among many. Here are some of their stories... .

In the early part of 1959, a church in the northern part of New Jersey invited Dad to bring some of the boys of Harlem to a men's dinner. But Dad's boys didn't have the right clothes to wear; they each had to go around to two or three houses before they found appropriate coats, shirts and ties. Once they got to the church they said they had never seen so much good food; they each had two or three helpings.

As things turned out, the speaker to the men's group that night was a presiding judge from the court in Philadelphia. His message centered on the difference between right and wrong and how we can be forgiven for our wrongdoing through Jesus Christ. When the judge gave the invitation the first to raise his hand was one of the Harlem boys, Shane. On the way home Shane confided in my father that he was supposed to have helped three friends in a robbery that night. Shane was glad he had gone to church instead.

Once the group got back to Manhattan, Dad picked up Captain Jensen and took the boys out for hamburgers; the boys were still hungry! Dad told Jensen about Shane's decision. The Captain

put his arm around the Puerto Rican boy and said, "Well, you know that makes us brothers now."

At six o'clock the next morning my father received a phone call saying that Shane had been picked up by the police on suspicion of murder. The night before, two police officers had surprised three youths in the course of a robbery on Lexington Avenue. One of the officers and one of the boys was killed. This was the hold-up Shane was supposed to have helped with.

By the time my father arrived at the police station, the chief detective was already questioning Shane: "Where were you at 12:15 last night?" Shane's answer was talked about for months afterward in the 23rd Precinct: "Sir, I was with Captain Jensen!"

Shane's new way of life was soon evident. Before, he had not been able to hold down a job; now he had a steady one. He started buying better clothes and renting a room to live in. Before his commitment to Christ he used to sleep outside on rooftops rather than go home to be with his alcoholic mother, and brothers who each had a different father. Like Eddie Suarez, Shane started memorizing Bible verses and helping to reach other youth for Christ in his neighborhood.

Another night in 1959, Dad had a Puerto Rican gang at 2110 going through an electronics class when the Red Wings, an Italian gang, came to declare war on the Puerto Ricans because they had cut through their turf on the way to the club. The seventeen-year-old leader of the Red Wings, dubbed Bambino, found an old broken chair in the alley and sent it sailing through the front window of the club. Bambino figured his gang would take the club by storm; he didn't count on the six-inch thick security wall inside the window. Next, the Red Wings tried battering down the front door. At first, the Puerto Rican gang had fun just watching the Red Wings' failed attempts at break-in on the closed circuit television, but then they got a little bit over-excited and ran to the YDI kitchen to grab butcher knives. Dad had a few uncomfortable

moments sandwiched between the hopped-up Puerto Ricans and the warmongering Italian gang. But when the Red Wings couldn't penetrate the front door they finally gave up and left.

The next day Dad sent word that he wanted to see the leaders of both gangs. He sat them down at a meal together and told them they needed to cool it. He reminded them that the club was neutral turf and that they were all welcome, at the proper times. Around the table that day the Puerto Ricans and the Italians became friends.

Bambino was one of fifteen boys who went with Dad to Pinebrook Bible Conference, Percy Crawford's camp in Pennsylvania. Bambino later reported, "On July 1st, I met Jesus Christ as my personal Savior. After two weeks I was back in New York. I've tried to get out of my habits. I'd like to have the other kids in the gang get saved."

Subsequently the Red Wings confided in my father that they had planned to bomb the club and take Dad's life. The change in Bambino and other events slowly won them over. After their leader's conversion they couldn't do enough to help my father.

Boys weren't the only ones to have their lives transformed. A girl named Nickie was another teen who had her life changed from the inside out when she found Christ at a meeting in New Jersey where Dad was speaking.

Nickie had come from a poor home and was leader of the Frenchie gang. She used to hang out on 100th Street, known locally as "Junkie's Row" because more narcotics were sold there than on any other street in New York City. In school Nickie threatened teachers and organized inter-school fights. But after meeting Christ, Nickie renamed her gang: Delightful Ladies. One of her new rules for the gang: members must go to church.

These are just three out of many success stories that came out of Dad's time in Harlem. Suffice it to say that out of the first nine boys my father worked with in Hell Gate, all nine accepted Christ,

and all but Santy Lopez, who died too young, went on to live exemplary lives as adults—from community leader to social worker to bakery foreman to engineer. In fact, the boy who led the largest gang, of over 900 members, went on to become a vice president with Chase Manhattan Bank.

38

The Need for a Camp

The Sunday school trips to Steinway Hall showed my father that these kids were ready for more outings. Dad became tour conductor as he took these young people to see things, practically in their own back yard, which they never knew existed—like the Statue of Liberty and the Empire State Building.

My father also wanted the kids from Harlem to see open country instead of concrete, a place where trees grew wild and kids didn't. That's how YDI's camping program began.

A friend of the ministry had a place in Croton-on-Hudson with some hills to hike and a small lake for swimming. Dad got the kids ready with sleeping bags and tents from an army surplus store. A church in Hawthorne, New Jersey had a food drive which enabled the first group of campers to cook their food in tin cans over an open fire. The only problem that first summer was caused by bugs; the kids named the place Mosquito Gulch.

After two summers, the property in Croton-on-Hudson was sold. Dad went on an all-out search for a new camp location—a place where he could eventually build his own facility. My father called a real estate agent and told him what he was looking for. The agent said he had just the place: an abandoned gravel pit in Glen Spey, New York. Dad didn't think the gravel entrance looked par-

ticularly enticing, but the attached sixty-acre lake and surrounding woods were beautiful. Timber for the gunboats of the Union Army had been culled from this site during the Civil War, but you would never have known it because in 1961 almost every inch of the 360-acre piece of property was again covered with trees.

There was just one problem: YDI could not cover the purchase price of $86,000. Dad asked for a three-month lease over the summer with an option to buy. Five hundred dollars got him a place for summer camp with the kids from Harlem for one more season. The YDI Board was a little leery of this project because Dad used the last $500 in the YDI account to cover the lease. Still, each of the board members agreed to pray that the Lord would provide the money to purchase the camp. They even made a commitment to each get up at six o'clock in the morning to pray for God's answer.

After Billy Graham came to speak at 2110 in October of 1960, Dad decided to have other special speakers address the club. Among them were: Jerome Hines of the Metropolitan Opera Company; Roger Hull, president of Mutual of New York; and George Champion, president of Chase Manhattan Bank.

Dad had met Champion at Billy Graham's New York crusade in 1957. Champion and Hull served as co-chairmen of that crusade. Even before they met, friends had suggested that Dad should contact Champion about helping with YDI. But my father was reticent to approach people he didn't really know, looking for a hand out.

He and Champion met again at a dinner meeting of the Protestant Council of New York. Mom and Dad were seated next to the Champions at dinner. Champion asked about Dad's work and my father told him briefly about YDI. They didn't meet again until Champion came to speak at Steinway Hall.

That night in Steinway Hall, Champion gave a sparkling verbal portrayal of his early life as a farm boy in Illinois and his climb to the heights of Wall Street. My father was later amazed that Champion had agreed to speak to the youth that night at all, considering

his schedule. While Champion spoke to the kids of Harlem, former governor and presidential candidate, Tom Dewey, was waiting in the limousine outside to continue on to the grand opening of Chase Manhattan Plaza.

A few months after the meeting at Steinway, my father was informed that YDI was being investigated. Someone was putting questions about Dad to a judge in family court with whom he had worked, as well as quizzing Flax, Gersh and Jensen. Then late one night Dad heard a knock on the solid oak door of 2110. He checked the television screen but didn't recognize the man at the door until he announced himself over the intercom. It was George Champion.

Champion was on his way home from a trip to Washington DC and he stopped by for a chat. My father gave him a tour of Hell Gate. When they came back to 2110, Champion put his feet up on the desk in the office and asked, "What is your greatest need?"

My father quickly shot back, "A camp." Then he proceeded to tell Champion of the beautiful 360-acre site in upstate New York.

"How much?" was Champion's next question.

Dad responded, "It will cost $86,000 to purchase the property and another million dollars to build the facilities we will need."

Then Champion offered, "I'll cover you for the $86,000 and I'll see what I can do about the million."

From that time on, Champion took responsibility to raise the money to purchase the camp. He asked to come on YDI's board, in order to establish an official tie with the organization. Any other group would have voted him on in a flash. But the current members of the board wanted to make sure that Champion's views on the Christian faith would coincide with their own. It required a glowing recommendation of Champion from Billy Graham to convince the board two months later. It was just as challenging trying to add two other board members Champion wanted on the project: John B. M. Place, a former vice president of Chase and later president of Anaconda, and Donald L. Wallace, an attorney,

who would later handle the fund-raising directly. However, the old board members soon warmed up to the new men when they saw how dedicated they were to helping YDI.

Champion proceeded to invite key friends and leaders from New York's financial community, eight or ten at a time, to luncheons held in his private dining room at Chase Manhattan Plaza. Dad was to give informal talks about his work in Spanish Harlem. At the first meeting, my father looked around in awe of these tycoons and wondered what he was doing there. He felt especially humbled in the presence of Tom Dewey, whom he remembered waving from his car in Los Angeles during his presidential campaign in 1948. However, Dad began to relax when he realized that, though these men dressed in the best suits, they were just like other people on the inside. Eventually my father met the leaders of forty of the largest corporations in America. Many of these Wall Street wizards were more than politely generous toward YDI. Ten and fifteen thousand-dollar checks were not uncommon. But the checks that startled Dad the most were ones of a more moderate amount that came from a friend of George Champion: President Dwight D. Eisenhower.

39

Into the Wild Blue Yonder

While George Champion did all he could to raise funds for Camp YDI, Dad also had to do his part. This meant going on the road again, this time to raise funds.

Dad didn't have a lot of spare time in those days, despite the fact that he would regularly get up at four o'clock in the morning. The only other way he could save time was through transportation. Traveling by car from Tarrytown to then Idlewild Airport (later JFK) took too much time. Then there was the waiting for a flight. So my father decided to purchase, and fly, his own plane; in the end it proved more economical than traveling on commercial airlines.

First, Dad had to learn how to fly and see if he liked it. He absolutely loved it. Within a few months he was a licensed pilot and had bought a small, single engine Piper Cherokee. Having a private plane cut hours off of travel time. Dad eventually traded in the Piper for a twin engine Cessna that was somewhat larger and therefore safer for night flying and longer journeys. By that time he was "instrument rated." I still remember the number on the plane: N10JV. Whenever Dad would call to the tower he would say: November One Zero Juliet Victor. How striking that he would pick the date he never made in St. Louis to be the number on his plane, now that he was flying with and for the Lord.

After Dad started flying to various speaking engagements, a friend in Tarrytown mentioned that a neighbor, Paul Wheatley, enjoyed flying and might just like to join him for the ride. Paul was a notary and Dad had used his services in the past to notarize papers for YDI. He called Paul and asked him to join him on a plane trip. I'm sure Paul had little idea what he was getting into.

In one year, Paul and Dad made over one hundred different stops, mostly sandwiched between Friday and Sunday nights. There were a few mid-week trips. When they would arrive at their destination, Paul would play the part of advance man and make sure things were properly set up for Dad to speak. If Dad was planning to use his electronics, Paul would make sure all the equipment was there and set up correctly.

Paul also got Dad out of a lot of "coffee and conversation" sessions. Not that there was anything wrong with that sort of thing. It was just that after flying non-stop from who knows where and then speaking and participating in Q&A afterwards, Dad was usually exhausted. Paul would say just loud enough for everyone to hear: "Hey Jim, I know you don't want to leave but the weather up north looks likes it's getting worse. If we don't leave in the next couple of minutes we might not make it to our next stop." Often Dad had meetings scheduled two hours apart and two hundred miles away from each other, so he and Paul were always on the move!

Dad also learned how to travel light. He would take a shaving kit and briefcase with clean shirt, a second pair of underwear and fresh socks enclosed. If he had to, he would also take a second suit on a hanger. On one trip Dad was scheduled to talk to a small group in a Chinese restaurant in Los Angeles just minutes after landing. There wasn't time for Dad to stop and change clothes anywhere else so he wouldn't look rumpled. Dad commandeered the restroom for a couple of minutes while Paul stood watch.

As the fund-raising efforts of my father and George Champion bore fruit, Dad was happy to tell his real estate agent that he was

ready to purchase the 360-acre piece of property. The day he came home from signing the papers, Dad saw our neighbor, Larry Parrish, in his driveway. He called to him, "Hey Larry, we got our camp for the kids!"

"That's great Jim, where is it?"

"Oh, you probably never heard of it. It's in a little town called Glen Spey, New York."

Larry cut Dad off and led him into his house. "Jim, I want you to meet Miller Fagley from Glen Spey."

My father was amazed. As they exchanged names, Dad learned that Fagley was a contractor. "Do you build houses?" he asked.

"Yes."

"Can you build a camp?"

The conversation was hurtling rapidly toward a business deal until Dad informed Fagley he didn't have all the money to build just yet. But he set up an appointment with the contractor in Glen Spey.

At the appointed time the two men met, my father–the large and loud man from the city, and Fagley–the neat, trim, thoughtful and entertaining conversationalist, puffing away on his pipe. They sat together beside a country road and Dad outlined his vision for the camp. From their first meeting they were able to communicate with each other wonderfully.

The opposite was true of the architect Dad hired to draw up plans for the buildings. So Dad fired the architect and Miller Fagley did the building design himself. He and Dad drew sketches in the sand by what was to be named Lake Champion. There seemed to be just the right spot for every building they would need.

At a Camp Champion reunion some thirty years later, Miller Fagley said to the group gathered there: "I am sure that every one of you, at some time in your life, met a man who made you outdo yourself. This man would inspire you to do better than you could possibly do. And as far as I'm concerned, Jim Vaus was that man."

40

Camp Champion

At the dedication of what was to become Camp Champion, an air of peace was felt during the prayer. Harlem kids were quiet, eyes closed, during the moment of reverence. Delighting in that sacred silence, Dad opened his eyes and looked up in order to impress on the film of his memory the faces of those young people in prayer. The holy hush was interrupted for my father by the sight of a young girl, stark naked. She was taking advantage of the moment, with everyone's eyes closed, to change out of her bathing suit into dry clothes!

Another moment Dad never forgot, and always enjoyed telling about, was the first time George Champion visited the camp. The tour of the property was going smoothly. The food was excellent. After lunch Dad took Champion for a short walk down the hill to the lake. A New York thunderstorm caught them out, halfway down to the shoreline. Dad and Champion were soaked through to the skin. My father began apologizing for marching Champion out into a rainstorm when suddenly a brilliant rainbow appeared at the end of the lake. Champion turned to my father and said, "Seeing that rainbow has been one of the most beautiful moments of my life. It's all the proof I need that this camp is what it should

be." Thus our future home at the end of the lake was later named Rainbow's End.

In the very early days of YDI, my father acted as camp director, chief cook and bottle washer. The kitchen was a large open barbecue pit down by the lake. One day Dad was flipping hamburgers for a large number of hungry teenage mouths when a visitor strolled over. Dad put him to work flipping even more burgers. By the time they got around to formal introductions, Dad found that the man he had employed at the barbecue was Alan Betts of the Astor Foundation, a friend of George Champion. Dad later took Betts off hamburger duty and gave him a tour of the property, showing him where they planned to build.

A week later my father got a phone call from Alan Betts. He said he was impressed with the camp and the way it was being operated. Then he offered a contribution of $300,000. Dad started adding up in his head what was needed to meet budget and consequently told Betts, "YDI isn't ready for $300,000." Dad asked for $150,000 instead. Betts couldn't believe my father refused half the money; no one had ever done that before. But Betts gave what Dad asked for nonetheless. In the end, when my father was ready, he called Betts a year later and asked for the rest of the $300,000. Betts laughed, but Dad got the other $150,000!

Contributions, large and small, from people across the nation made Camp Champion a reality. One of those small gifts came from my Grandma Lillie.

From the time that my father was born, his mother always believed and prayed that her son would go into the ministry. During the years that Dad was involved in criminal activities she never gave up hope. One of her greatest joys in the last years of her life was the fact that my father was finally involved in Christian work.

She and Grandpa Jim visited our family in New York shortly after the camp was purchased when there were as yet no buildings. Those were the days when our family stayed in a trailer at camp.

Grandpa Jim and Grandma Lillie came for another visit when camp was under construction and very close to completion.

Grandma kept saying to Dad that the one thing the camp still needed was a chapel. She said she couldn't help financially toward the building, but she wanted to give some money toward a pulpit Bible and perhaps some of the furnishings for the chapel. When she returned home after that second visit she sent my father a check for $150.

Shortly thereafter, Grandma Lillie died. My father knew she was dying, but he had to stay in New York for a very important event ... my birth. He stayed in Tarrytown until I was born, then he flew back to California to see his mother before she died. Grandma Lillie hung on until Dad got there to see her, then she passed away—just two days after my birth.

After her death, Grandpa Jim found some money tucked away in a secret compartment of Grandma Lillie's desk. It wasn't very much. But she had saved very diligently, a little money at a time. With the cash was a note saying that if this was found after her death the money should go toward the building of the chapel at camp.

Dad shared that story with a Mr. and Mrs. Cordes who then gave the first large gift of $1000 toward building the chapel at Camp Champion. They told Dad to add their gift to what his mother had given.

My father had asked Mark Hatfield if he could get some lumber for him to build the chapel, since he was Governor of Oregon, a state with a huge lumber business. Dad got a telephone call some time later from a Jewish man named Robert Seaman who said, "Governor Hatfield wants me to come up and see your camp and see if I can't be of help to you in giving you the lumber for your chapel."

Bob Seaman from Tidewater Lumber Company on Long Island came up to see the camp. He asked Dad how much lumber he would need. And Dad said, "I just happen to have a list right here."

In the summer of 1967, after the chapel was completed, Dad hosted a Bob Seaman Day at camp with a dinner and all the fancy

trimmings. Bob Seaman showed up ... with his Rabbi! After Seaman helped with the lumber, the Cordeses gave another contribution, supplying the rest of the money that was needed to finish the chapel.

It was alone in that chapel in the summer of 1976, at the age of thirteen that I committed my life to go into Christian ministry. Grandma Lillie had a good vision. But little could she have known what her vision would bring about in her own family.

41

Miller Fagley

Over the years Camp Champion developed into a combination of manicured village, blended with natural wilderness, tended by Miller Fagley's expert hands. Miller is an amazing man who grew up in a small town in Pennsylvania and as a young naval officer landed on the beaches of Normandy on D-Day. Miller and his wife Dottie, the postmaster of Glen Spey, became part of our family in many ways. Growing up on the east coast, away from extended family, I referred to the Fagleys as Uncle Miller and Aunt Dottie from my earliest years.

The dining hall was the first building Miller and his team constructed at camp. It sits atop a grassy knoll, which slopes gently down to the shore of the lake. The kitchen inside was top-notch with five commercial size ovens, long sinks and enough supplies to feed an army. I especially enjoyed the walk-in refrigerator and freezer in which a deer carcass would invariably be hanging in late autumn. The chef back then was Henry Bosch, former chef to General George Patton.

The original cabins at Camp Champion were set up in villages nestled in the woods just the other side of the lake. Miller re-created an early New England covered bridge to connect the villages to the main part of the camp. The wood was taken from a neighbor-

ing dilapidated barn built in 1790. When the kids from Harlem needed a raft to float on the lake, Miller manufactured the U.S.S. Tom Sawyer.

Miller designed it all, including the Lodge, Chapel, Springbrook (a house for visiting VIPs), the Recreation Hall, Administration Building and Rainbow's End. Even the railings around the porches on some of the original buildings are extraordinary, containing silhouettes of arrows pointing toward heaven. One day when Dad asked Miller why he created the railings with that design, he replied: "Isn't that what this place is all about, pointing people to God?"

It took Miller a while to decide to become the manager of Camp Champion after he constructed the first buildings. He and Dottie had a young daughter, Kathy, and they were nervous about her being around the delinquents from the city. But my father had ingenious ways of talking people into things.

One day Dad said to Miller, "I want you to design the perfect house with all the facilities needed for a resident manager."

"Okay," Miller agreed.

"Another thing," my father continued. "I would like the house to be ready before the end of the year. Be sure that there's a fireplace, a good kitchen, and comfortable rooms. Just go to it."

Miller did. And when he was finished Dad said, "How about moving your family in for Christmas?" Miller did move in with his family and remained as resident manager throughout YDI's years of operating Camp Champion.

One of my favorite stories involving Miller Fagley took place the day my father was at Camp Champion and received a letter from one of his former clients, J. Paul Getty. Dad had contacted Getty, asking him for a contribution toward the work of YDI. Dad strolled over to where Miller was standing in front of the Administration Building and said, "Miller, I have in my hand a letter from the richest man in the world. I wonder what size contribution is inside." Dad opened the envelope and found a check for $25.

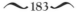

Faster than you could say "Jack Robinson", Miller Fagley got out his checkbook and started writing a check to YDI. My father queried, "What are you doing, Miller?"

"I'm writing a check to YDI for $30. I want to be able to say that I gave more than the richest man in the world!" Miller really did give more than the richest man in the world to make Camp Champion a reality, not only financially and in terms of his time and talent, but in other ways as well.

The people of Glen Spey thought it was great for there to be a camp for poor kids from the inner city, but they wished it wasn't in their community. Some were scared. One woman wouldn't even use the road that passed in front of camp. She would take an alternate route that went far out of her way. Other people were downright nasty. During early construction, the "Lake Champion" sign was torn down and in its place was put a sign which read: "This way to the tax-free n***** camp." The bottom line was the community did not welcome YDI, so Dad started a campaign to win them over.

The most influential man in that campaign was Miller Fagley. He was well known and respected in the community. Miller and a local insurance man invited some of the townspeople to dinner as camp guests. After the meal Dad told them he had heard the rumors floating around, that an ex-gangster was opening a camp for delinquents from the city. Though that was true, Dad tried to convince the crowd that it wasn't as bad as it sounded. He shared his life story and then cast the vision of YDI. My father assured people from the community they wouldn't see city kids running wild through town; they had enough room for them on the 360-acre campsite. Dad didn't win any enthusiastic support that night, but it bought him some time to prove to the community that YDI could fit into life in Glen Spey.

Youth Development did its best to be a part of the community. As a tax-exempt organization they didn't have to pay local taxes, but

YDI made contributions to the volunteer fire department and the highway fund anyway. Slowly, Dad earned Glen Spey's respect.

The most important thing was that Camp Champion had a powerful impact on the lives of inner city youth. Prior to camp, the most that these kids had seen of the wilderness was Central Park. At camp these teens learned how to swim, canoe, and handle themselves out in God's creation.

One moonless night two camp counselors were taking a group of kids on a hike through the woods. The leaders stopped for a few moments to decide which trail they would take back to camp. The kids walked on. Suddenly they realized their leaders were not with them.

"Where are we?"

"How do we get back to camp?"

"What was that noise?"

The counselors caught up with the boys and listened in on the conversation waiting to see what these young men would do. Finally, one guy said, "Let's pray." The counselors were silently thrilled. A boy named Felix was elected to say the prayer: "Please God, help us out of this darkness. Lead us your lost children, back to camp safely." Each boy added his own "Amen." After a golden moment of silence one voice pierced the darkness: "O.K., now what the **** do we do?"

42

Trouble on the Street

YDI wasn't successful with every boy or girl who came their way. In January 1963, tragedy struck. Four YDI boys–Tony, James, Steve and Teddy were walking down Second Avenue when a city youth board member, Lou Marsh, stopped them. In those days members of the city youth board were assigned to various streets to try to keep the peace. Apparently Lou Marsh suspected these boys of being on their way to a gang fight and he wanted to talk them out of it. However, the only fight in sight was stirred up by Marsh's intervention.

The boys told Marsh there was no fight going down and one of them pushed him out of the way saying he was not their youth worker and he was not a cop. Marsh stepped back in front of the young men and somewhere along the way one of the boys slapped him. Then Marsh raised his fists, rigid in front of him, as though he was going to fight them. The boys of Harlem knew only one way to respond to this, so Steve hit Marsh first. Lou's body became rigid and he fell backward, the sound of his head hitting the pavement was like a cracking watermelon. Marsh never regained consciousness; he died two days later.

My father got involved immediately. He tracked down the location of the boys and got the real story out of them. What came out

later in the trial was that Marsh was an epileptic and that he often had episodes where he would raise his fists rigid in front of him. Furthermore, Lou Marsh had no marks on his body other than those caused directly by the seizure and the fall. Dad knew by the way each of the boys told the story, independent of each other, that something didn't sound right. He figured they were guilty of getting into an argument but not much more. Dad realized that if these boys didn't get proper legal representation they might all go down for murder. YDI decided to employ legal counsel to defend them.

The news media exaggerated the story of what these supposed hoodlums had done to Marsh; reporters said that the city youth board member had been beaten, stomped, chained and clubbed. Various news reports swayed public opinion in favor of the dead Lou Marsh.

In the course of the trial, the District Attorney tried to paint as black a picture of these young men as he could. He even put my father on the stand and dragged out the negative parts of Dad's past, hoping to smear YDI. At the end of the trial, the judge instructed the jury that if they thought the action of the boys in any way caused the grand mal seizure then the boys were as responsible for Marsh's death as if they had physically beaten him. All four boys were convicted of manslaughter and sent to jail.

YDI kept in touch with each of the boys while they were in prison. Two of the young men obtained their high school diplomas while incarcerated. When the four got out of prison, they were paroled into the custody of YDI. Dad arranged for two of them, Tony and Steve, to attend King's College in Briarcliff Manor, New York; YDI footed the bill. Unfortunately, another one of the young men, Teddy, later died of an overdose.

My father's ministry in New York City not only changed the lives of young men like Tony and Steve; it changed his life as well. Dad's understanding of people and ministry deepened. When he was a traveling preacher in the 1950's, some of his messages could

be very pointed, bordering on judgmental. I think Dad's experience in New York made him much more tolerant of many different lifestyles while still holding on to the essentials of the Gospel.

Dad came to look at people's problems in a way different from what his fundamentalist background would have dictated. Whereas some looked at alcoholism or drug addiction as purely sinful choice and nothing more, my father began to look at these problems as sicknesses in need of psychological, as well as spiritual help.

In short, Harlem taught my father to deal with the whole person in ministry: physical, emotional, intellectual and spiritual. YDI evolved four basic thrusts: health and recreation to meet physical needs, guidance and counseling to meet emotional needs, remedial and tutorial education to meet intellectual needs, evangelism and Bible study to meet spiritual needs. Dad was no longer interested in just gaining decisions for Christ. He didn't want to continue playing the "Protestant Numbers Racket" as he called it, whereby the success of ministry would be measured by the thousands of people you could win to Christ. My father became much more concerned with the individual and making sure that individual was grounded and growing in Christ in all dimensions of life. He was truly a shepherd who had found lost sheep and now wanted to help those sheep become nourished in all ways.

43

A New Problem

As I mentioned earlier, my father had polio in the early 1950's. As a result, he walked with a limp for the rest of his life. In the mid 1960's, Dad developed another medical problem—diabetes. Eventually he had to give himself daily shots of insulin. But in 1969, at the age of fifty, my father noticed yet another problem: a tremor in his left thumb.

Without warning his thumb would involuntarily punch an imaginary button. In time Dad felt a quiver in the thumb, almost like an electric current. Soon enough this undesired movement was a daily occurrence. Dad's general practitioner sent him to a neurologist. The specialist shook my father's right hand, then his left. He asked him to plunk out a tune on the piano. Dad's right hand did fine, but he lost the rhythm with his left hand. Within five minutes the neurologist diagnosed the problem as Parkinson's disease.

The doctor assured my father that no one ever died of Parkinson's, but on the other hand, there was no known cure either, short of a brain operation. Brain surgery had worked for some but not for all. Dad did his own research and learned of a man who became a complete vegetable as a result of the operation. That was only one case, but Dad didn't want to take the chance. He settled for medication, which didn't accomplish much. The tremor spread.

At that time a new medication for use with Parkinson's patients was being tested at the Albert Einstein College of Medicine in the Bronx. The drug was L-Dopa. The only people who could take the then experimental medication were part of the college's research program. Dad applied to be part of the program, but he was turned down because the doctors in charge said they were only accepting "hardship" cases. My mother wrote a letter to the college insisting that my father was a hardship case. She explained a bit about his medical history, then communicated in her letter what kind of work my father was doing in the inner city and how much other people depended upon him. Mom's letter opened the door for Dad to the testing program and he was put on L-Dopa.

The winters in New York suddenly became treacherous for my father. He frequently lost his balance and fell on the icy streets. His doctor cautioned that if he broke a bone on the left side of his body during a fall, it might not heal properly since the tremor wouldn't leave his body still long enough for the bone to mend. The physician didn't say my father had to move out of snow country, but he did say that if he were facing the same problems personally, he would move to a warmer climate. For Mom and Dad that meant moving back to California.

My parents decided on San Diego as the place to settle. Dad's sister Virginia and her husband Jim lived there, and San Diego didn't have the same smog and overcrowding that was starting to overtake Los Angeles. So in January 1971, our family moved to a house that my parents bought in La Jolla. La Jolla means "the jewel" in Spanish, and at the time the village of La Jolla was just that, a jewel in greater San Diego, perched prettily on the coast.

Early in the 1960's, my sister Madeline had been diagnosed with a mental illness, which required long-term hospitalization. This was a heart-wrenching experience for our whole family, the details of which could fill another book. Suffice it to say, when our family moved back to the west coast, Madeline needed to stay in a hospi-

tal in New York. Dennis was finishing college at Houghton, and Steve was starting at Eisenhower College, so my brother Roger and I were the only ones to make the move to California with my parents. Nonetheless, Mom and Dad bought a five-bedroom house overlooking the Pacific Ocean with enough room for Dennis and Steve when they wanted to visit. While the move was the best option, really the only option for Dad, it was still difficult for Roger and me, changing schools and cultures. But eventually we adapted.

The one really positive thing about Dad's Parkinson's was that he spent more time at home and we all got to spend more time with him. Even with L-Dopa, it got to be very tricky for my father to step smoothly on to a platform and stand speaking for long periods. Plus the tremor became embarrassing to him when it spread throughout his left arm. When under any amount of tension or nervousness, as in public speaking, Dad's arm would just start to move sporadically and he couldn't control it. In addition, as the Parkinson's developed, he just couldn't think fast enough on his feet. So his speaking engagements decreased.

Though I have happy memories of growing up in New York and being at Camp Champion, my memories of Dad from that period are mostly of him being gone, or of him coming home from a trip. Dad used to leave his shoes by the front door when he came in the house. I had nightmares about those empty shoes, and Dad not being there to fill them. But now that we were beginning a new life in California, my father was there to fill those shoes and be a real Dad at home, just as he had been a father figure to so many in Harlem.

Before the move back to California, Dad suffered one more loss. His own father, Grandpa Jim, died on May 3, 1970. It is the only time I ever remember seeing my father cry.

I'm sure Dad felt like he was running on empty. During the previous ten years he had lost one daughter through death, and another to mental illness; his mother died shortly before my birth;

now his father was gone too. But the emptiness in Dad's heart was no longer an infinite abyss. Soon enough the Lord was filling him up again so that Dad could spend the last twenty-seven years of his life passing the overflow of the love of God on to others.

PART FOUR:

Overflowing

(1971-1997)

44

Summit Expedition

While Parkinson's disease was not a life-threatening illness, it did make my father question how long he might live. At the time of the move to California, my parents' only financial asset was their home in New York. Dad prayed that he might live long enough to see his family better established financially.

To that end, my father was desirous of working out his own financial support and not being dependent upon YDI as we made the move to California. With that in mind, my father started a company called Processed Medic Data (PMD) in order to provide computer services to doctors and others in the medical field. Unfortunately, this business failed, but was replaced by two others: Coast Computer Corporation and Coast Video Corporation. Coast Computer was a consulting business in the computer field; Coast Video was a TV production house for making features, commercials, covering sports events, both in the studio and on location. With both of these companies Dad saw some moderate success.

While my father was developing innovative endeavors in business, his mind was no less motivated with creative ideas for ministry. He explained some of those ideas in an interview with *The Wittenburg Door*, for their February/March issue of 1971:

I'm not an old man, but physically I can't do all the things I could before. I'm putting my money, so to speak, on getting hold of people with real talent and real ability and making it easy for them to do the job. I think we have a lot of talented young guys today coming out of seminary and college that have a good background and their head screwed on right. And given an opportunity, they could develop a very outstanding ministry. I think the role I see myself in is kind of Mr. In-between. I would like to see to it that the resources are provided so that guys like that can carry on a ministry. Maybe a one-man ministry or maybe along comes a guy with a vision for a larger task that embodies several. I think so often dollars and cents are the limiting factor to what can be done and I think that I can pull together the dollars and cents through the organization we have. And I'm looking for talent.[13]

One of the young, talented men my father discovered and launched in ministry was Tim Hansel. The ministry Dad helped to start was called Summit Expedition.

For several years a young man named Gary Templin had been the director of Camp Champion. Gary wanted to broaden his knowledge and he was very impressed with Outward Bound, a wilderness adventure camping program for youth. So eventually he left YDI and went to work for Outward Bound, becoming its director in Colorado and establishing the work in California. My father was very interested in Outward Bound but he felt the thing it was lacking was a Christian emphasis. Dad thought the wilderness mountaineering and adventure program would be a great setting to introduce young people to a personal relationship with Jesus Christ.

Dad hired Gary Templin to find a man with the appropriate experience and Christian character to launch a Christian version of Outward Bound. Templin found just the right man in Tim Hansel. Tim had been a halfback at Stanford University, graduated with a Master of Arts degree and later coached football at Stanford. Tim

also taught science, psychology and history at the high school level. In addition, Hansel had experience as a Young Life leader and instructor for Outward Bound; he once bicycled all over Europe and sailed 25,000 miles around the world in a forty-foot sloop!

The activity of Summit began at a base camp in the high Sierras of northern California. Kids would carry their bedding and supplies on their backs and make meals out of cheese, pilot biscuits, honey and packets of dehydrated food revived with water. From base camp, Tim and his team would lead groups of teens hiking into the Sierras where they would learn how to climb mountains, rappel off of them, and basically develop all the skills necessary for survival in the wilderness.

Tim created an atmosphere of encouragement on every Summit Expedition excursion. After climbing up a sheer rock face teens couldn't help but be proud as they looked back at what they had accomplished. The atmosphere of Summit allowed teens to shed their masks and take a real look at their lives. Fireside chats probed spiritual issues. During these seminars in the wilderness, individual kids learned that they weren't alone in their experiences of life. In the group context many had a chance to discover the ultimate way to live through a relationship with God.

My brother Roger was fifteen years old when he went on one of the first Summit trips in the summer of 1971. He went to the mountains still a boy, but came back a man–literally. His hair and beard grew long so that he really fit into the hippie crowd in the early 70's. Roger, who had always struggled with being overweight, came back from the Sierras slim and trim. But more importantly, he came back from the mountains with a new friend–Jesus Christ.

Eventually the ministry of Summit Expedition spun off on its own with Tim as leader. He went on to become a best-selling author and speaker on the Christian lecture circuit. Nothing could have made my father happier; he was achieving his goal of reproducing others who could carry on unique ministries to youth. Dad

knew that through this kind of multiplication of ministry, he could reach many more young people than he could by just working and speaking by himself as one lone voice.

As our family life got firmly rooted in California, Dad was disturbed by the fact that he wasn't able to give sufficient leadership to the YDI ministry and outreach in New York. At first he tried flying to New York twice a month to oversee operations there. But he was only able to give a "lick and a promise" to the work in the east.

The immediate answer to the problem was for my father to replace himself in New York. He did just that when he hired Alec and Rita Rowlands. Dad met this dynamic couple at a youth rally in Ohio. Alec, who had completed work on his Master of Arts degree in urban geography, was serving as youth pastor at St. Clair Avenue Baptist Church; Rita was directing a musical group. Dad first sent Alec and Rita to observe and report back to him on YDI's ministry in New York. My father was impressed enough with the Rowlands' recommendations to make Alec the new executive director of the work in New York. Under Rita's capable leadership YDI formed a music group, Master Design, which traveled around the United States giving concerts and advertising the ministry of Youth Development.

In the end, however, Dad couldn't keep burning the candle at both ends. He ended up dissolving the New York YDI operations and giving the camp and inner city work there to David Wilkerson's ministry, Teen Challenge. Meanwhile, the Rowlands joined the new YDI in California while Dad turned his attention to fresh and innovative ways of reaching youth across America.

45

Television and Radio

My father did not use Coast Video Corporation for secular business purposes alone. For a while in the early 1970's, he pioneered a new kind of Christian television program. It was called *Tell It All*, based upon the title of a hit song by Kenny Rogers and The First Edition.

"I never watch it–I don't understand what they're talking about." Those were the words Dad was hearing from young people talking about Christian television programs. Those words struck a responsive chord in my father's heart. How could the television media be used to effectively communicate with the un-churched young person of the early 70's?

There were some important ingredients to the kind of program my father had in mind to fill the gap. The content of the show needed to be fast-paced, capturing and keeping the attention of the viewer. The message of Christ could not be compromised.

The end result of some intensive planning was a television format dynamically designed to reach America's un-churched population. YDI television crews would go out on location and capture the excitement of a stunt pilot spiraling to the ground, film a group of young people on a Summit Expedition excursion in the High Sierras, or cover a music festival with over 15,000 in attendance. Dad wanted

to show life in action but also demonstrate how life could be transformed by the power of Jesus Christ. *Tell It All* also included a talk show segment with my father engaging youth in conversation and telling his story of transformation from gangster to gang-buster.

Tell It All was a great idea, attuned to the times, but it was destined to have a short life. Dad was able to get the program on to the Armed Forces network for a period of time. But the cost of putting the show on regular TV stations around the United States was prohibitive. So my father turned to a less expensive medium–radio.

In the 1970's, according to one report, 99% of America's youth were tuning into a rock radio station every week. That report set the wheels in my father's brain turning. Here was the chance to touch the lives of thousands of young people. YDI's REALITY radio network provided the vehicle.

In 1974, REALITY appeared for the first time on secular stations all over the United States, the same year that Dad had his second autobiographical book published: *The Devil Loves a Shining Mark*. At first, REALITY had a format of 85% music and 15% talk in thirty and sixty minute lengths. Over time, that combination was changed to 99% music with a 2-minute message and an offer of follow-up counseling and literature. My father employed full-time counselors to answer thousands of letters each year from young people looking for someone to listen and care. Eventually Dad got over 200 secular, rock radio stations across the country to air REALITY every week.

How did he do it? Dad knew that secular stations were required by the Federal Communications Commission to reserve some airtime each week for religious programming. So he hired staff to design a high-quality program secular radio stations would accept. REALITY used three different formats in four programs per month. The first format was pre-evangelistic. Themes might cover such topics as: Is There a God? What is Christianity? Or the theme might be something as simple as Loneliness. The second format was designed to present the whole Gospel message. The REALITY disc

jockey would give teens a chance to respond to the message and accept Christ as their leader and forgiver. The third format was for new Christians. The disc jockey would make suggestions about how to begin and grow in a relationship with Jesus Christ. Each young person responding to the program would receive a follow up letter and be enrolled in the Billy Graham Evangelistic Association follow-up course.

REALITY got positive reviews from individual Christian leaders and secular stations alike. But more importantly, it touched the lives of young people in a profound way, young people without hope just as my father had once been without hope. A young person from Washington State wrote to YDI:

> *I heard your program for the first time this morning on KISW and I was very interested. I never gave Jesus much thought before this. The program gave me a different outlook on life.*

Another wrote from Oklahoma:

> *I'm 16 and I've been into dope pretty heavy the last few months and I really would like to get off of it but I feel my life is lacking something, maybe GOD.*

And yet another young person, this time from Lincoln, Nebraska contacted YDI:

> *I need Christ. I'm scared about tomorrow. I want Jesus wall-to-wall. Please send me anything you can to help me.*

Clearly YDI was touching a chord with REALITY. But even as this radio program was coming into being, Dad was becoming aware of another frightening reality on America's horizon: runaway teenagers.

46

Reaching Out to Runaways

A national tragedy etched itself on my father's mind in August 1973. Graves were discovered, piled high with the bodies of teenage boys in Houston, Texas; Dad wondered what was happening to the rest of the homeless children of America who might become victims just like those boys in Texas unless someone did something to help them. After all, Dad had run away himself more than once, so he could identify with the problems of runaways.

My father discovered that teenagers were running away from home in epic proportions; one million destitute teenagers were on the run every year. These homeless youngsters were from every segment of society and from all races. The average age of a runaway at that time was fifteen years old. It appeared there was no meaningful agency in operation to help or minister to these young people.

According to an NBC special, San Diego County was a center for drifting teens attracted to the warm climate and happy-go-lucky lifestyle of Southern California beach communities. Having no place to go, runaways would seek shelter in places like cemeteries or laundromats, or simply hang out on the streets. They would become targets for drug pushers and hustlers. Girls would be de-

fenseless against sexual assaults. And when caught by authorities, runaways would be treated like criminals.

Dad received information from San Diego County's chief of probation and the heads of juvenile hall and juvenile court, telling him the runaway problem was getting worse. At that time there were only two homes for runaways in the county. One could handle six kids and the other eight. The police department told my father that they had a steady stream of seventy kids with nowhere else to send them but to detention facilities.

With all of this in mind my father decided to establish, through the ministry of YDI, a place for runaways. He called it Samaritan's Ranch. It was a five-acre miniature version of Camp Champion, complete with a lake and twenty adjacent acres available for expansion. Sam's Ranch was located in El Cajon, California and initially there were two houses on the property, a horse barn, corral and one other building. There were acres of open space with fruit, avocado, evergreen and deciduous trees. The ranch-style setting eventually allowed youth to participate in gardening, learning about fruit trees, and raising a calf.

Dad's goal was to expand to the point of being able to accommodate at least seventy young people, along with foster parents and staff who would follow the example of the Good Samaritan from Jesus' parable. My father's intention was to provide a place where runaways could begin to have their emotional wounds healed and be nursed back to health before being returned to their parents. In cases where parents would not offer love and care for their children, YDI sought to take over the job by providing foster care and guidance under the supervision of the courts.

By this time Dad was accustomed to being a pioneer. In New York, before the days of civil rights' protests and marches, he had to confront people, especially in the church, with the need for social outreach. Now in California my father was trying to stir up interest

in lost and lonely teenagers with long hair and different lifestyles. The bottom line was that Dad was trying to live according to the challenge of the New Testament:

> What good is it, dear brothers and sisters, if you say you have faith but don't show it by your actions? Can that kind of faith save anyone? Suppose you see a brother or sister who has no food or clothing, and you say, "Good-bye and have a good day; stay warm and eat well"—but then you don't give that person any food or clothing. What good does that do? (James 2:14-16, NLT)

Sam's Ranch evolved into being more than just a home for runaways. YDI began to provide residential care and treatment for emotionally disturbed youth of all kinds. Initially, Sam's Ranch accommodated six adolescents, ages 14 to 17. Children with mild emotional disturbances, some acting out, pre-delinquents, those with minor criminal offenses, truancy problems, as well as runaways were among the target group.

The Ranch provided lodging, board, supervision and rehabilitative treatment on a 24/7 basis. It offered social living, education and therapy. The environment engendered reasonable structure, secure living and an opportunity for emotional honesty. The teens Sam's Ranch served had seldom seen the like. The Ranch became a place for self-discovery and positive behavioral change for many young people.

Dad brought together a capable staff in order to make Samaritan's Ranch a reality. The initial staff included an administrative director, two couples as house parents, a social worker, a psychologist, a consulting physician, a dietician and a caretaker. Additional consulting staff in remedial education, vocational programs, agriculture and handicrafts, were also made available.

The accomplishment of Sam's Ranch could be summed up in the story of one boy. His name was Ronny. When he came to Sam's

Ranch the staff wondered how such a handsome young man with a football player physique could have sunk so low in just sixteen years of existence.

Ronny was deeply involved in the drug culture. His only goal in life was to play in a hard rock music group. He was dirty, rebellious and angry. He was full of hate, disillusionment and failure.

It wasn't easy for any of the staff at Sam's to love Ronny at first. Many prayed again and again that God would help them to react with love towards him as Ronny made things very hard on the staff as well as his peers.

Over time, Ronny began to see in them something he had never experienced before—honest caring. And the staff exposed him to a family he never knew existed—the church. At a church meeting one night several other boys responded when the invitation was given to accept Jesus Christ as leader and forgiver. Though Ronny's heart was beginning to melt, his will still didn't budge.

The next day, Ronny's house parents began talking to him about Christ and the important place Jesus should have in his life. Somehow that personal conversation helped Ronny to yield his life to God. He knelt on the kitchen floor with his house parents and asked Christ to forgive him of his sin and take control of his life.

In the days that followed, the change in his life became evident. When the church youth group asked him to be their piano player, even though he didn't know the Christian songs and hymns, he gave it his best. When it became known what was taking place, someone donated a piano so Ronny could learn the songs and practice them at home.

There was another change too. From that time forward whenever the house parents would check on Ronny in his room they would find him alone, reading the Bible that had been given to him. He began to love the One whom he used to curse.

By the time Ronny reached age eighteen, he was ready to leave Samaritan's Ranch. He had a job and had saved money for the first month of rent on an apartment. More importantly, he was grounded in a personal relationship with God. In Ronny's life everyone could see the fulfillment of the vision of Sam's Ranch—life transformation through the power and love of Jesus Christ.

47

Never Enough Room

Sam's Ranch eventually expanded to include multiple group homes in suburban settings. Each home at one time had swimming facilities and some even had horses. Most importantly, each home provided loving care with proper discipline and training and was licensed by the State of California to care for six boys. Therapy would begin with the mother-father role and the establishment of a strong home and family environment.

The boys at the ranch were eventually offered a unique experience in which to participate on weekends or holidays. YDI was given a new facility in the summer of 1976, Jewel Valley Ranch or "Mission of the Jewels" as Dad liked to call it. This 160-acre site, fifty miles east of San Diego, provided the setting for boys from Sam's Ranch to enjoy an experience in adventure-centered education. Here the boys were taught the art and value of gardening, cattle-raising and animal husbandry. In addition, they experienced a learning adventure in backpacking, survival skills and teamwork similar to Summit Expedition.

Sam's Ranch started working in conjunction with federal and local training and employment programs to provide paid work experience where boys would be given the opportunity to learn a skill. There were a wide variety of opportunities for boys to choose from.

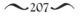

Dad would drop in on occasion and teach electronics to the kids, just like he used to do in Harlem.

The Ranch developed a program to train boys approaching the age of 18 to make the transition from the ranch to the world of work and self-responsibility. The staff at Sam's would make sure individual young men, like Ronny, were established in a job and making mature decisions as they moved toward self-sufficiency.

From the time that my father opened the doors of Sam's Ranch, however, there was one major problem: lack of sufficient space. There just wasn't enough room for all the boys who needed the kind of help Sam's Ranch could provide.

That's why, in 1978, YDI entered into a contract and eventually bought Green Valley Ranch, a property already in operation as a twenty-four hour residential care facility. On a beautiful fifty-four acre site outside of Ramona, California, fifty more boys could be given a chance at a life they had never had before. The opportunity to purchase Green Valley came along just in time, because by the autumn of 1978, YDI was forced by disgruntled neighbors to move out of Sam's Ranch.

There was just one thing that bothered my father about Green Valley. Because the ranch received government funding, there was a stipulation that religious activities could not be required as part of the program. Dad continued to provide Christian guidance and activity to the youth at Green Valley through the house parents, staff, visiting speakers and groups, as well as through coordination of services with local churches. But some of the kids who most needed to hear about God's love would not participate in these services because they didn't have to.

Green Valley enjoyed great success, but the scope was limited. This was true for two reasons. One was simply size. The other problem was that Green Valley was licensed by the government to serve only those children fourteen years of age and younger. The vast

number of young people, ages fifteen to eighteen, who were sitting in juvenile hall, were excluded.

Dad started having the probation and welfare departments of several western states clamoring for his attention. At one point there was a waiting list six months long of teenagers needing to get into the program YDI was operating. My father figured YDI could fill another two treatment facilities immediately, if he could raise the funds to purchase, furnish and staff them.

In the summer of 1980, once again Dad found just the right place. It was known as the Ahern Ranch in Valley Center, California. My father quickly renamed it Paradise Creek Ranch. It had enough housing for thirty more young people. Actually, Paradise Creek had five homes complete with furnishings, one small schoolhouse, one vocational training building, and one treatment center on its twenty-three acres. YDI was able to get it all for $273,000.

To troubled youth caught in the turmoil of those times, Paradise Creek Ranch was a real paradise. Peering out from state operated institutions, detention facilities, juvenile halls and jails, more than 300,000 young people were looking for the kind of hope and opportunity Paradise Creek could provide back in 1980. Granted, this new ranch would only make a small dent in the overall problem of juvenile delinquency, but at least it made a dent. For each of the boys accepted there, Paradise Creek was like a light at the end of the tunnel. Boys who had never seen a horse had the chance to care for one. Like at Sam's and Green Valley, there would be time for crafts, art, work and study. Paradise Creek helped to turn boys into men and led them into the discovery of what it means to have real worth and a new lease on life.

Between two ranches and sixteen homes, by 1980, YDI was providing, not only room and board, but complete physical, emotional, educational, vocational, medical and spiritual care for 97 boys, 24 hours a day, 365 days a year. YDI was the largest provider of residential care and treatment for boys in San Diego County. Some-

times Dad said he felt like the old lady who lived in the shoe, he had so many children he didn't know what to do. With almost 100 boys and 75 staff it took a lot of planning to make the dollars go around. But with God's help, the work continued year after year.

48

Christmas in Juvenile Hall

The problems of juvenile delinquency were growing so rapidly during the 1970's that the court systems of the United States were falling further behind with each passing year. Young people were sitting in juvenile detention centers with little hope for the future. No one seemed to care.

But Dad cared. And he wasn't content to reach only as many youth as he could house at Sam's, Green Valley and later Paradise Creek. So he devised a ministry to reach many more youngsters trapped in detention centers.

Dad knew what it was like to be sitting in prison over the Christmas holiday. What could be bleaker? So he came up with the idea to reach inside of juvenile detention facilities with a loving hand, sharing a simple gift of a T-shirt, a letter and a book telling about Jesus' love for all, regardless of circumstance, location, or life history.

My father approached juvenile authorities in San Diego and got a rough estimate of how many kids for whom he would need to prepare gifts. On Christmas Day, the packages were delivered to Juvenile Hall in San Diego along with an invitation to seek him out if there was any way he could be of help.

The response was so overwhelming that plans were made to reach into more juvenile detention centers across the country the

following year. The gifts would still be delivered personally, in many cases by a staff of dedicated workers. I remember one year flying with Dad to Albuquerque, New Mexico to deliver packages to juvenile offenders there.

One year the gift YDI sent drew a tremendous response from kids across the western states. It was a specially designed T-shirt with the slogan "Movin' Up" along with the name of their city emblazoned on the front. The letter accompanying this gift suggested that the young person write YDI for more information if they wanted to "move up" with a new life for the New Year. Dad also wrote a very special booklet entitled "Love" that went into the gift packages over a number of years.

One note, from a boy named Jerry, arrived the day after Christmas in 1980. It was typical of the heartbreak that came to Dad's attention through the mail:

Dear Jim,

I have read your book "love" It's a very good book. I never thought about love in thoughs ways. I want to learn more about Love. Like how to show my mom I love her. I know she loves me but she don't show it. So Tuesday I whent out and stole a car. Now hear I am in Juvinial Hall and will be going to court on the 26th and will be locked up for about 1 - 1 ½ years some place. If you have the time I would like for you to come see me and Talk to me about my problems with Love. Yes I do belive in god and have been babtised to the Morman church but have not atended for about 5 Years now. I want to learn how to go to church with my mom and my two brothers and stick with it. Im not a bad kid but my familly needs help showing their love we just don't know how to get along when we don't. I'm 16 and I'm realy not a bad kid. Yesterday I was suposed to start Job training school and I blew it. Now I don't have any hope no more and think about suiside. Almost every minit I think about how can I kill myself but theres

know way to do it in hear unless I take a dive head first to the flore but if I don't die I'm gona have a sore head. But after I read "Love" I felt better as if god him self gave me that book. But I was woundering if you can help me and my mom live together without fighting I love her so much and would like to have some counsling with her and I can't because I'm in hear and will be locked up somewhere for a year or so. I was wondering if you can get me help. Because being locked up isn't going to help me but going to church and love in god will. Well today is Christmas and I've been praying alote but don't think its going to help me out none. I want to get out of hear go back to school and church. and start the new year out right and make something out of my life I don't want to spend my life in Prison I need help now so I won't. Well we have to go to our rooms again. I hope you get this letter and will come and talk to me because like I said suiside is all I think about. Thanks for helping Jerry

How would you respond to a letter like that? It was just one of many my father received that year from kids in juvenile hall, but Dad felt he had to do something more about this one. So he went to see Jerry.

As my dad described him, Jerry was a handsome, fine looking lad. But he appeared tense and nervous, and his hands shook. Jerry said, "I really didn't think you would come." Before Dad left he told Jerry he would talk to his probation officer and see if he could arrange to have the court send him to Green Valley Ranch or Paradise Creek Ranch for care and training.

My father had several more meetings with Jerry at Juvenile Hall. In March of 1981, Dad got a call from the judge saying that he would like to place Jerry with YDI for treatment. In April, my father wrote to supporters saying:

I am rich today because a boy ran to meet me ... he put his hand in mine, smiled and said, "I made it." Little did Jerry know

about the work that had gone on behind the scenes. The Judge and a few others thought he ought to go to prison; "after all this wasn't the first car he had stolen." The light within Jerry's eyes told me of his happiness here at Paradise Creek Ranch. I tell you Jerry's story because he is but one of 97 boys; each story has a similar sound. Each story is a miracle in itself. My prayer is that in this experience each boy will be resurrected, born anew.

If it wasn't for YDI's Christmas Outreach, Jerry might have given up. If it wasn't for my father going to visit him, Jerry might never have seen the love of Jesus fleshed out. And if it wasn't for Paradise Creek Ranch, Jerry might never have had a new shot at life.

Over the years, YDI's Christmas Outreach grew by leaps and bounds. Nine years after its launch, it was reaching into juvenile detention facilities in nineteen states with a message of Christmas hope. Thousands of young people were hearing the message that Jerry had heard: "Jesus loves you."

49

Mattie Stewart and Home Echo

To help many boys like Jerry required money. Over the years my father became an expert at fund-raising. But he also showed a great deal of integrity in that part of his life and ministry.

One day in the 1960's when we were still on the east coast, my father got a call from a Mrs. Mattie Stewart in Columbus, Ohio, who had been a regular but modest contributor to the ministry of YDI. She said that she was coming to New York and she asked if Dad could meet her at the airport. My father was tied up with work in the Tarrytown office, and so he asked a staff member to greet Mrs. Stewart at the airport and give her a tour of YDI's work in New York City. When the staff worker dropped off Mrs. Stewart at the airport after their tour, Mattie Stewart gave the staff worker an intriguing message to pass on to my father. "I had something to give to Mr. Vaus, but now he'll have to come see me to get it."

Some months passed with no further word from Mrs. Stewart until a call came from a man who said he was her pastor and that he was coming to New York. He had something to deliver to Dad from Mrs. Stewart herself. The pastor wanted to be met at the airport, but he specified it had to be my father who would meet him. Dad drove through the snowy winter weather to meet what turned out to be a very distinguished looking African American pastor. At

the pastor's request, they drove together from the airport to Camp Champion in the Catskill Mountains of New York, a three and a half hour journey.

When they arrived at camp the pastor was awestruck by the loveliness of the place. Cordes Chapel was beautifully snuggled in a fresh layer of snow, surrounded by evergreens heavy-laden in a mantle of white. Dad took the pastor into the chapel and as they walked down the center aisle the pastor said, "I guess this is as good a place as any to do business." With that the man pulled from his overcoat a wad of money–fifty-dollar bills, hundred dollar bills, and one thousand dollar bills. The total reached $100,000.

Now Dad was awestruck! Not knowing what else to say, Dad assured the pastor, "I'll see that our treasurer sends Mrs. Stewart a receipt for this immediately."

The pastor responded, "Oh, you send receipts do you?"

"Always," Dad replied, "whether the gift is large or small."

"Well then, here is another $200 I had in my Bible for safe keeping."

Sometime later Dad went to meet Mattie Stewart in person to thank her for this most generous contribution. Mrs. Stewart was an elderly African American woman, somewhat small in stature, and obviously keenly interested in the work of YDI. When Dad met her she told him she needed his help–to count some more money she wanted to give to him! After counting what appeared to be just the beginning of an avalanche of cash, Dad realized that to protect this woman, and to protect himself, they ought to have an attorney and a certified public accountant present. My father could just imagine the headlines if he didn't take such a precaution: EX-CON SWINDLES WOMAN OUT OF LIFE SAVINGS.

Within a few days, the presence of the CPA and the lawyer were arranged, and the counting began afresh. It now became clear that Mrs. Stewart had little trust in banks. She had all of her money stashed away in shoe boxes and under mattresses, in jars and the like—proceeds from a retirement home she ran called Home Echo.

When all was said and done the total amount came to approximately one million dollars. And Mattie Stewart wanted to give it all to Dad.

Though YDI could have used the money in many ways, Dad refused to accept the donation. He said to Mrs. Stewart, "You know what people will say? They'll say, 'That big white man took that little black woman for all her money! What a shame!'" Mattie Stewart persisted; she offered that she would leave the money to YDI in her will. My father was still concerned about the whole deal, but he contacted a lawyer for Mrs. Stewart and the will was drawn up.

However, it was later discovered that Mrs. Stewart had run into financial difficulties with her nonprofit corporation. So Dad helped Mattie Stewart to set up a trust fund for the retirement home. As a consequence, YDI never saw one penny of Mrs. Stewart's fortune. Mattie Stewart has since passed away, but Home Echo for the Elderly was able to keep up its operation, thanks to Dad.

One other large donation was offered to YDI about ten years after the incident with Mattie Stewart. This time a well-dressed woman in her early thirties came into YDI's offices. She wanted to speak with my father about her aunt who was quite wealthy, and near death. The young woman expressed that it was her aunt's desire to leave her vast fortune to Youth Development.

A few days later the young woman returned with the money–in cash, stocks and bonds, totaling over a million dollars. After speaking with the young woman's aunt by telephone my father felt that the elderly woman was in full control of her faculties. He agreed to accept the donation on this occasion. YDI deposited the cash, leaving the stocks and bonds in the woman's name, at least for the time being. And my father took one further precaution–he left the cash unspent, safe in a special YDI account.

Dad's caution later proved to be quite wise. Bank of America moved to have the elderly woman declared incompetent and suc-

ceeded in recovering her donation to Youth Development, along with interest!

Both of these incidents displayed my father's God-given wisdom in handling money. It is no wonder that YDI was one of the charter members of the Evangelical Council for Financial Accountability, along with about one hundred other Christian organizations. YDI was one of only two such organizations in San Diego that belonged to ECFA in the early 1980's. As my father said in an interview with the San Diego Tribune in 1981, ECFA "grew out of a desire to make sure that evangelical Christian organizations meet higher standards of accountability to the public. We believe it's an excellent thing and brings a greater degree of integrity into the touchy part of this kind of work." Indeed, ECFA has achieved that goal and I am proud of the fact that my father was in the forefront of that movement.

50

Father and Sons

In June of 1982 Dad wrote to all of the YDI contributors saying:

> I am pleased to tell you that two of my sons are active in the
> work of YDI. Will directs our new program for grade school chil-
> dren called Youth Advantage. Steve directs our new radio series
> called This Is It. In addition to this Steve is accepting a limited
> number of speaking and singing engagements (representing YDI).
> All of us continue to marvel at the transformation Christ brought
> into his life. Our God is great!

Youth Advantage was born out of a need I discovered while
teaching Sunday school at our home church. I began to realize
how many children in the church were growing up in homes where
mother and father were divorced. It seemed to me that providing
an adult mentor for such children would be critical to their devel-
opment, both emotionally and spiritually.

I did some research on what the Big Brothers organization
was doing in this area, and then developed my own Christian
Big Brother/Big Sister organization, sponsored by YDI. From lo-
cal churches we recruited adult mentors for children ages seven to

fourteen, mentors who would spend a few hours per week with an individual child for a minimum of six months.

All volunteers had to go through a screening process which included application, interview, evaluation of interpersonal relationship skills and fingerprinting to make sure none of the adult mentors in our program had any incidences of child abuse or molestation. I also did the training of volunteers in how to minister to children from broken homes. I developed the initial training and ongoing monthly support sessions for our mentors based upon books that I had read and training I received in counseling.

We received referrals of various children in need of a mentor from counseling agencies and churches throughout San Diego. Some of the kids we worked with had learning disabilities; others had behavioral difficulties or had been abused. Some were just looking for an adult friend to spend time with them. It was a somewhat modest project carried on while I was a full time college student, but at least we were able to help a small number of families in the San Diego area.

My brother Steve had been working as a free-lance singer/ songwriter, playing nightclubs when he committed his life to Christ after seeing a Billy Graham program on television. After that commitment in 1981, Steve eventually started working for YDI in 1982. He pioneered a new radio program for Youth Development called *This Is It*.

Steve's principle in producing the show was simple and based on an opinion he had held since first hearing REALITY. Whenever he heard YDI's old radio program he couldn't help but think that thousands of radios clicked off as soon as the first Christian song hit the airwaves. At any rate, Steve's radio was always one of the first to click off! So his idea was to use the music that was popular on all radio stations and weave the Christian message in and out of those songs. While Steve believed that contemporary Christian

music was popular with Christians he felt that it had no market with the people he wanted to reach: non-Christians.

Not all of the stations that carried REALITY came over to *This Is It*. Just as REALITY was being phased out, the Federal Communications Commission lifted its requirement for each station to provide free public service time. In light of that decision, many stations switched to doing only in-house programming. Still, *This Is It*, like REALITY, was heard nationwide.

In the autumn of 1983 we were invited, as a family, to sit on the platform at the Billy Graham Crusade in Sacramento, California. Steve sang one of his new Christian songs that night. It was a thrill for Mom, Dad, Steve and me to be together at that crusade and listen to the man who had brought so much positive change to all of our lives.

One funny incident took place at the crusade that night in Sacramento. While Dad was talking with someone else on the platform, a man came up to Mom, Steve and me and asked us how our father was doing. Mom couldn't resist telling Dad later on that someone thought she was his daughter! The fact of the matter was, Mom was ten years younger than Dad and always looked younger than her years. Dad took the comment in stride.

51

Home Run

In 1981 my father was asked if he would give some technical assistance to the Redlands Police Department. Ever since his conversion in 1949, Dad was always eager to help various police departments in any way he could. He volunteered not only his help but the skill of the boys at Paradise Creek Ranch. It was a rare opportunity for these teens to work for rather than against law enforcement.

If you drove by the Youth Development offices in San Diego in 1982, you would have seen the result of Dad's labor. Dad and the boys of Paradise Creek transformed a Blue Bird bus into a thirty-seven foot police vehicle for helping officers in distress. It was called "Code 99." It was, at the time, the most sophisticated, state of the art, electronic communication center on wheels. The police were shouting the praises of YDI for its design and construction. It was written up in many police journals. Dad was most excited because it provided a real hands-on educational experience for the boys from the ranch.

Ed was one of those boys. He had taken part in Dad's first electronic clock building project. When he came to work on the Mobile Command Center, Dad started Ed out punching hundreds of wires on the main frame of the telephone system. Ed was quick

to learn the color codes for a 25-pair cable. When Ed was released from probation he asked if he could continue to live at Paradise Creek and work for YDI. Dad said, "We'll take you."

On May 3, 1982, the Senate of the California Legislature passed a resolution commending Dad and the boys of Paradise Creek for "Code 99." The Mobile Command Center rolled out in the Fourth of July Parade in Redlands. Ed was just one of many proud boys who had a part in making that police vehicle a reality.

The Mobile Command Center for the Redlands Police Department worked out so well that Dad did a similar "Code 99" project for the police department of Escondido, California. He was honored with a plaque from that city on March 18, 1987.

Dad also played a key part in the forging of the San Diego Crime Commission. The purpose of the Commission was to improve criminal justice in the city on all levels, including juvenile justice. Once again, my father raised the necessary funds and hired the right staff to carry out the project–including a high-ranking official from the Federal Bureau of Investigation. On October 11, 1984, the newly formed Crime Commission honored Dad with a Distinguished Citizen Award delivered to him at a large banquet held at the San Diego Convention Center. The speaker for the evening was William Webster, director of the FBI. The plaque read:

> To James Arthur Vaus, Jr.
> A True Servant of God
> You Have Given Your Every Strength
> To Youth and Your Community

Never a truer word was said.

During the time that my brother Steve and I worked for YDI, Dad came up with yet another idea for helping troubled teens. He was still concerned about the one million runaways on the roadways of America every year. And he wanted to do

something more about it than what he was able to do through group homes.

My father decided to start a nationwide runaway hotline. Nothing like it existed in the United States in 1983. I remember asking Dad one day: "But how are you going to advertise the hotline and get kids to call in?"

I'll never forget his answer: "I don't know. But we're going to do it." It was at that point I realized what a visionary my father was. Before that time I always figured Dad had the answer to just about everything. He didn't. He just acted like he did. He was always stepping out in faith, trusting God for the answers. And that faith inspired others to get on board with him.

Of course one of the first things Dad did was to share his new vision with YDI contributors. One thing he was not going to do was accept government funds to run the hotline. He had had enough of government intervention in YDI's group homes. In fact, it was that intervention which finally led my father to get out of the group home business shortly after starting the Home Run Runaway Hotline.

Dad went about designing a computer system to handle calls from runaways. He had someone on the YDI staff compile a list of over five hundred shelters around the country to which YDI could refer these lost and lonely teenagers. He made a deal with one of the major bus lines in the nation to provide free transportation home for every youth in need. Then once everything was set he started advertising the hotline any way he could. He got free listing of the hotline in telephone books across the country, plus public service announcements on over five hundred radio and TV stations throughout the United States.

From the outset YDI didn't have enough staff to handle an abundance of calls 24/7. But that was alright because we didn't have that many calls coming in. The immediate solution was to have existing staff at YDI handle the calls. As low man on the

totem pole, I got the job of handling all calls after office hours. I didn't sit at a computer terminal all the time. Instead, I went about my normal schedule, carried a manual around with me listing the five hundred shelters across the United States, and I wore a beeper. Sometimes I would get a beep as I was driving down the freeway. I would have to stop, find a payphone, and call the office or our answering service to retrieve the call. That was long before cell phones became popular! At night YDI's answering service would simply call me at home.

When I started answering calls in January 1984, the hotline was only averaging a paltry five calls a month. But within six months we were receiving over a thousand calls per month. I was regularly awakened in the middle of the night by a call from a runaway teenager in some part of the country. Quite often the situation wasn't as simple as just referring them to a shelter. In many cases the young people calling needed someone to talk to about their problems. Many of them were alone, afraid and contemplating suicide. Others were trying to eke out an existence as male or female prostitutes. Still others had run from abusive home situations to which they couldn't return. Consequently, I did a lot of listening and praying, offering hope and counsel as best I could. In most cases the youth who were calling had no idea they were talking to someone only a few years older than themselves.

By June of 1984, we all realized the influx of calls was way more than I could handle. We went about training some twenty-five volunteers who took over the job I was doing. Very soon the Home Run Runaway Hotline received national media attention in print, television and radio. The hotline went from a thousand calls per month to six thousand calls per month. By the end of 1987, the number of calls mushroomed to over twenty thousand calls per month, a 250% increase over the previous year. YDI was able to get many of those callers to shelters, provide food and clothing, and in some cases, where appropriate, reunite parents and children.

But the biggest need Dad was facing by that time was where to get enough Christian counselors to handle the calls. My father little knew it at that time, but his answer was literally just around the corner.

52

Passing the Baton

As Dad approached his retirement years I know he prayed and pondered a lot about who would take over YDI after he was gone. It was my father's desire that one of his sons might lead Youth Development into the next generation and the next millennium. But it wasn't like Dad ever told any of his sons what they should do for a living. He was always quite circumspect about that. He made sure we got as much education as we were willing to go through, and he tried to open as many doors of opportunity for us as possible, but he never pushed or dictated exactly what direction our lives should take.

By 1985, my brother Steve had migrated back to the music industry where he eventually became quite successful as a singer, songwriter and producer. His studio was at one time the largest recording studio in San Diego.

Just before I went off to seminary at Princeton, my father turned to me and asked if I would be interested in taking over the leadership of YDI after I finished my schooling. I told him I wasn't sure and that I would have to pray about it. I really wasn't sure that I wanted to wear my father's mantle; I thought, perhaps, that the Lord had something else in mind for me. In the end, my father helped me to establish a nonprofit corporation for the

purpose of supporting my own Christian ministry of preaching, teaching and writing.

But while I was away at seminary, other possibilities began to percolate. My brother Roger, who had been wandering from the faith for a time, began to attend an exciting church in San Diego called Horizon Christian Fellowship. Horizon soon became the largest church in San Diego, reaching some six thousand people every weekend and spinning off daughter churches reaching thousands more. Roger invited Mom and Dad to come have a look-see. On visits home from seminary I attended Horizon with them. It was indeed a dynamic church. Packing out a junior high school auditorium to standing room only, Horizon had several services. The music was contemporary, upbeat and very professionally presented. The solid biblical messages from Pastor Mike MacIntosh were relevant and refreshing. We saw many people coming to personal faith in Christ each Sunday.

When Roger discovered Horizon and Mike MacIntosh, my parents were thrilled with what he had found. Despite the fact that the congregation didn't sing any of the old hymns, my parents loved it. Eventually, Roger introduced my father to Mike, and Roger wondered from the beginning whether there might not be in Mike a potential successor to my father in the work of Youth Development. As Dad and Mike got to know each other, eventually discussions about YDI came up and Dad asked Mike to pray about taking over the ministry. Mike did pray quite earnestly about it, and after a ministry trip to Eastern Europe, Mike came back with his answer.

Mike MacIntosh took on the leadership of YDI, initially keeping the offices at the Ruffner Road facility, but eventually moving them to Horizon's facility at Mt. Alifan Road, only a few blocks away. Dad remained on the board of directors for YDI, thus insuring a smooth transition. Most importantly, what Mike was able to do with the hotline ministry was absolutely phenomenal. Through his connections with Calvary Chapel pastors and congregations

across the United States, Mike was able to develop a vast pool of volunteer Christian counselors to staff the telephones. And Dad designed a software system to route the calls to various churches across the country.

Under Mike's leadership the hotline expanded from just handling the problems of runaways into truly being a National Youth Crisis Hotline. YDI started utilizing the gifts of Christian young people across the country as hotline counseling volunteers to reach hurting kids with the good news about God's love; Mike called it Teen Talk. Advertisements for the hotline also multiplied through billboards, public service announcements in theaters, even appearances on the Good Year blimp.

YDI also continued some of its other ministries like the Christmas Outreach into juvenile detention centers nationwide, wilderness expeditions and its Aid to Youth Fund. Mike creatively expanded the ministry of Youth Development in a number of ways such as offering Thanksgiving dinner to thousands of youth in shelters across the country, the Ready for Action Team bringing professional Christian athletes to speak at school assemblies and other events, and Easter/Spring Break Interventions deterring youth from alcohol and drug abuse on school campuses and at vacation hot spots around the nation. Under Mike's leadership, Youth Development Incorporated became Youth Development International reaching children and youth for Jesus Christ in such diverse places as Mexico, Grenada, Scotland, the Philippines, Canada and Russia.

My father was thrilled to say the least and he continued to be involved as the Chairman of the Board of YDI. His own words at the time described the transition best ...

"I still work on the design and implementation of software at YDI, together with staff volunteers scattered across the nation. Though 'retired', I still spend 10 to 12 hours a week in a corner of our home, where I have my desk and computer. The computer ties

me into the YDI network. It is a thrill to 'listen in' on some of the emergency calls. They come in such humongous numbers.

"Silently monitoring one conversation, I prayed for the 13-year-old girl who, between deep sobs and tears, told one of our telephone volunteers her story of sleeping in the bushes alongside a road. She was pregnant and scared. She was sure no one cared for her. What a joy to hear our loving volunteer share God's love in Jesus Christ!

"I think the high divorce rate, the shrinking number of mothers at home, drugs, parental abuse and godlessness is responsible for the great majority of tragedies we encounter. Our national hotline has become a personal '911' emergency service for American youth.

"YDI President Mike MacIntosh and his staff are performing above and beyond my expectations in assuming the reins of leadership. We could receive as many as a half million calls a year moving into the 1990's."

53

Dad at Home

I have spent most of this book telling you what my father was like in public life, but I think I should take some time before the close to describe what he was like in private.

First of all, Dad had a great sense of humor. One story well conveys my father's penchant for fun. During the days that my parents attended South Hollywood Presbyterian Church they became friends with Dr Cliff Hanna and his wife Edie, who later went as medical missionaries to South Korea. Cliff was a dentist and my parents went to his practice for all their dental needs. Cliff, like Dad, had a great sense of playfulness about him. So one day while he was finishing up work on my mother he said, "You know, I've always wanted to do this ..." and he sprayed Mom in the face with the water gun dentists usually use to rinse out your mouth!

Not long after that, Mom and Dad went out to dinner with Cliff and Edie. Suddenly, in the middle of the meal, my father got a very serious look on his face, as he sometimes could. (Remember, his family called him Judge.) Dad got this very somber look and he said to Cliff, "I heard about what happened to Alice in your office." Quick as a wink, Dad picked up his glass of ice water and shot the water at Cliff. Unfortunately, Cliff was too fast for Dad and ducked. The ice water hit the lady in the next booth who was

wearing a dress that was very low-cut in the back. Dad and Cliff had a hard time explaining that one! But Dad loved telling the story for years to come.

I have some very early memories of my father; in fact my wife insists that I can remember the day I was born. It isn't true. But I do remember my father getting up very early in the morning at Camp Champion, waking me up, changing my diaper, and taking me down to the barn to feed the burro.

During our summer vacations at Cape Cod, Dad never came down to the beach with us. He disliked lying in the hot sun, and though he loved swimming in a pool, I don't remember him ever going in the ocean. He took me on other fun outings at the Cape however–like miniature golfing–or early morning trips to the donut shop. We used to eat the donuts on the way home and he would always make a game of it saying, "Please don't eat the hole!" I always did.

Dad was always a soft touch when it came to my wanting things. I can remember him buying me a board game I especially wanted from the toy store in Tarrytown. He would often play checkers with me when he was at home. And whenever he came back from a trip there was always a present in his suitcase. One time the present was a Mexican sombrero that I treasured for years to come.

Disneyland was a favorite place that Dad enjoyed taking the whole family to see. I think our family must have been one of the first ones there when Disneyland opened in 1955. Dad had a way of making every journey extra fun; he must have picked up his teasing habits from his father. He wouldn't ever tell us, "We're going to Disneyland today." Rather, he would say, "We're going to see Dr Neydis!" My brothers were very disappointed on my first trip to see "Dr Neydis." We all flew out to California together from New York and we stayed at the Disneyland Hotel but I came down sick in the middle of the trip and we had to return home early.

Dad spent a lot more time at home after he was diagnosed with Parkinson's and we moved to California. When he swam (always in a pool, as I mentioned), he had an amazing ability to float, literally on top of the water. It was quite astonishing to look at his large frame, the hump of his stomach, and even his toes sticking out of the water!

Dad was a great game-player. He and Mom loved playing Scrabble together. When we lived in New York, he would often play chess with Miller Fagley late into the night. And one Sunday after we came home from church in California, Dad taught me how to play poker! That was one of his favorite things to do with all of us boys. And yes–there was betting involved. Only Dad had such a soft heart he never felt right about walking away with any cash won off of his sons. He would always play until we were even or had won something off of him. That was always hard for Roger, who was an outrageous better and had some incredible losing streaks.

My father was great at taking naps whenever he was at home. It seemed he could fall asleep anywhere, in any position. I remember one time when I was about ten-years-old he fell asleep on the deck of our boat. I went to wake Dad up with a nudge, but Miller Fagley, who was with us on that excursion, told me not to bother my father. That was the first time I learned that Dad was someone special, worthy of respect and appropriate treatment. Today I know for certain that my own father is the greatest man I have ever known.

54

Head Waters

By 1995 I had been married for seven years with one child and one on the way. We were living in Columbia, South Carolina and one day I got a call from Mom and Dad. "We're moving to Virginia."

"You're what?!"

"We're moving to Virginia. YDI has been given a piece of property in a place called Head Waters. Roger is going to develop it into a youth camp and we are going to move there with him and his family."

Once I picked myself up off the floor, I was able to regain my equilibrium long enough to ask, "And where exactly is Head Waters?"

"It is somewhere just west of Staunton and Harrisonburg, Virginia, off of Interstate 81."

"I have a map of Virginia here. I'm looking at it very carefully and I don't see Head Waters."

"Well, it's there," Dad said, "It's a very small place."

"It must be." I replied.

Within months my parents, along with my brother Roger, his wife Lorrie and their almost one-year-old son, had moved to Head Waters, Virginia. What had happened was this: Elizabeth Kubler-Ross, famed author of the book *On Death and Dying*, had been operating a lodge in Head Waters which she hoped to use to serve

AIDS patients. After running the lodge for a period of time, Ms. Kubler-Ross decided to dissolve the non-profit corporation which ran the facility, thus necessitating that she give the property to another non-profit company.

Ms. Kubler-Ross made a nationwide search for the right non-profit to which she would donate the land and property. Working for her and on her board at that time were Paul and Betty McNutt, a couple who had a home in nearby Deerfield, and another home in California. When living in California, Paul and Betty attended a church in Valley Center, led by my brother Roger under the auspices of Mike MacIntosh and Horizon Christian Fellowship. So one day Paul and Betty said to Ms. Kubler-Ross, "You really should consider Youth Development, Inc. as the non-profit corporation to which you might donate this property." Ms. Kubler-Ross did just that; her corporation ended up giving that piece of property, with a seventy-bed lodge on it, and selling another 35-acre site with a house on it to YDI.

My parents moved to Head Waters in July 1995 and we visited them shortly after the birth of our second son that same month. When we first drove to Head Waters, on a gorgeous summer day, we couldn't believe how far off the beaten track it was. We kept driving and driving, wondering if we were ever going to get there. Once we had made our way over Shenandoah Mountain and down into the hamlet of Head Waters, we looked for the road to Roger and Lorrie's new house. If we had blinked we might have missed Head Waters itself, with the General Store on one side of the road and a 19th century clapboard Presbyterian chapel on the other side as the only landmarks.

At any rate, we made our way down route 616 and finally came to my brother's new house, one mile down the unmarked, two-lane road. As we drove up to the old log cabin style home we could hardly believe our eyes. There were Mom and Dad, Roger and Lorrie, waving at us from the porch, which also contained my parents'

washer and dryer at that time, since they had no other place to put it. Eventually my parents had their own house built on the same piece of property, right next door to my brother Roger, and at the end of a grass airstrip which my brother used for landing the YDI plane on a couple of occasions. The first day we visited my family in Head Waters they looked like they were already fitting into the rural lifestyle. But it was very hard to believe that my father, at age 76, had made such a move from San Diego, a city of two million people, to Head Waters with thirty people, most of them related in one way or another! Dad was like a modern-day Abraham, still responding to the call of God in his old age.

The next day Roger took us over to the lodge to show us what they had gotten into. It was in pretty rough shape, but you could tell that underneath was a beautiful facility; especially stunning was the two-story tall stone fireplace as the central feature in the dining hall. It reminded me of a miniature Camp Champion. That summer Roger spent most of his time getting the lodge into a physical condition where it would be both presentable and usable. And my family also hosted a luncheon to inform the community of YDI's vision for Head Waters Lodge. Everyone in the community was pleased that a Christian group was coming in to minister to youth.

By the following summer, Roger had the place up and running with a staff of people to handle the campers who came from various Calvary Chapel congregations up and down the east coast. The real feature of each young person's week at camp was the talk Dad would give to every group that came. Dad had done very little public speaking over the previous twenty years, but he felt called of God to share the story with these young people of how Christ had changed his life. Fortunately the lodge was equipped with a handicapped chair-elevator, which transported Dad to the second floor where the teaching and worship sessions were held. Even though he had to sit throughout his talk it was very moving to see Dad communicating Christ to young people again. I will never forget

one of the talks I sat in on and the number of young people who committed their lives to follow Jesus as a result. It was the last time I heard my father share his life story.

55

The Old Violin

Two years into the work at Head Waters, Dad was not doing very well; he had developed congestive heart failure. Then to make matters worse, early in 1997 he fell and broke his hip while trying to walk from his bed to his bathroom at home. He had to have an operation to set the hipbone back in place, followed by therapy at a nursing home. I'll never forget Dad struggling to walk again. Even with the help of a therapist and a walker, it was difficult. But I could see the look of determination in my father's eyes.

He had survived a scalding at sixteen months of age; he had triumphed through polio, diabetes and Parkinson's disease. So Dad wasn't going to let a little thing like a broken hip stop him. On Good Friday in 1997, I celebrated Communion with my parents in that nursing facility, but we were looking forward to Dad getting back home with Mom.

He did get back home and he did walk again, a little bit each day with the help of a walker. In October we had a small family celebration of my parents' fiftieth wedding anniversary. During fellowship around the table Dad again shared his hope that each of his four sons would be involved in the continuing work of Youth Development after he was gone.

In late November, I got a call from my brother Roger in the middle of the night. Mom had gotten up to check on Dad in his hospital bed, now installed in his own separate bedroom. She was unable to wake him, but he was still breathing. Mom called Roger who then called for an ambulance. At one point, while the ambulance was transporting Dad over the mountain, they had to stop. The emergency medical personnel were not sure that he was going to make it. Mom prayed, "Don't let him die here on the mountain." He didn't. They made it to Augusta Medical Center in Fishersville.

It was Thanksgiving week and I wondered whether I should go to Virginia to see Dad or go to my in-law's home in the Philadelphia area for a family Thanksgiving celebration as planned. I went to Philadelphia and kept daily tabs with the family. Dad wasn't doing well on Thanksgiving but by Sunday he rallied and was talking to the whole family. My mother kissed Dad goodnight on Sunday evening with a sense of relief.

However, the next morning when Mom came into the hospital, Dad looked at her and said, "I've asked the Lord to take me home." Mom asked what was wrong. She called in the doctors and nurses, but Dad soon fell into unconsciousness.

My family called me in Pennsylvania, where I was living at that time with my wife and two sons. Mom only had one word for me: "Come." We found someone to take the boys for us and we were getting in the car when we received a second phone call. Roger was on the other end of the line. "Dad died a few minutes ago."

Apparently my father's last word, during a moment of semiconsciousness, had been simply: "Snow." Mom told him there was no snow outside, that it was a beautiful sunny day. She asked what Dad was seeing but there were no other words.

Interestingly enough, when Roger phoned Mike MacIntosh to tell him of Dad's death, Mike reported a dream he had the night

before. He saw Dad playing in the snow with Dennis, Steve, Roger and me as boys. (I wonder if the first event after our reunion with Dad in heaven will be a snowball fight? Only the Lord knows.) Then in Mike's dream the image changed from snow to confetti—as Dad was surrounded by a large group of young people. Was his welcome into heaven a great party? Again, only the Lord knows, but it is fun to imagine what it might have been like.

What an appropriate way for my father to come to the end of his earthly journey. When I'm ready to go to heaven I'd like to be able to do what Dad did. I'd like to be able to say to the Lord, "I'm ready. Take me home." Perhaps an indicator of how closely Dad walked with the Lord is the fact that the Lord answered Dad's prayer in the affirmative on that occasion, for "Precious in the sight of the Lord is the death of his saints" (Psalm 116:15, NIV).

I have often thought about what my father's legacy is. He was certainly, and thankfully, much more than a gangster, even more than a gangster who got converted in a Billy Graham meeting. I believe Dad's legacy is simply this: that he passed on to others what he himself had received.

For his first thirty years, Dad was trying to fill the "infinite abyss" in his life with all sorts of things: electronics, wiretapping, working for a glamorous gangster. But none of those things gave him an ultimate sense of fulfillment. Dad's date with destiny—November 6, 1949—changed all that. That night in the revival tent, he received from the Lord Jesus Christ love, forgiveness of sins and fullness of life. My father then spent the rest of his life trying to fill the emptiness of others with that same fullness of God. The more he continued to give of himself, the more his life overflowed with love. Dad passed on the same gifts he had received from God to his own biological children and to countless spiritual sons and daughters scattered around the world.

Over the years as I heard Dad speak before groups, large and small, I would often hear him end his message by saying, "A poem

and I'll close." The poem he invariably quoted was "The Old Violin" by Myra Brooks Welch ...

It was battered and scarred, and the auctioneer
Thought it scarcely worth his while
To waste much time on the old violin,
But held it up with a smile.

"What am I bidden, good folks," he cried,
"Who'll start the bidding for me?"
"A dollar, a dollar," then, two! Only two?
"Two dollars, and who'll make it three?

"Three dollars, once; three dollars, twice;
Going for three ..." But no,
From the room, far back, a grey haired man
Came forward and picked up the bow;

Then, wiping the dust from the old violin,
And tightening up the strings,
He played a melody pure and sweet
As a caroling angel sings.

The music ceased, and the auctioneer,
With a voice that was quiet and low,
Said: "What am I bid for the old violin?"
And he held it aloft with the bow.

"A thousand dollars, and who'll make it two?
Two thousand! And who'll make it three?
Three thousand, once; three thousand, twice;
And going and gone," said he.

241

The people cheered, but some of them cried,
"We do not quite understand
What changed its worth?" Swift came the reply:
"The touch of the master's hand."

And many a man with life out of tune,
And battered and scarred with sin,
Is auctioned cheap to the thoughtless crowd,
Much like the old violin.

A "mess of potage," a glass of wine;
A game, and he travels on.
He is "going" once, and "going" twice,
He's "going" and almost "gone."

But the Master comes and the foolish crowd
Never can quite understand
The worth of a soul and the change that's wrought
By the touch of the Master's hand.

EPILOGUE

How can I describe the loss of my father? My mother put it best when, on the night of his death, she said: "He left behind a large hole." It was a surprise to me when I went to see his body laid out in the funeral home—how small that body appeared to be once his spirit was gone! I suddenly realized my father was "larger than life", not because of his physical size, but because of the infinite and immutable God who had come to fill his life, starting in 1949. Consequently, when he died he did leave behind a very large empty space.

I never knew before that I could shed so many tears. I cannot tell you the number of times over the past many years I wish I could have turned to my father and sought his advice, or simply heard his laugh. Then at other times I have felt as though my father is still very much alive. And so the hole he left behind is not an infinite abyss, for as the Apostle Paul once said: Christians do not have "to grieve like the rest of men, who have no hope" (1 Thessalonians 4:13, NIV).

We buried my father's earthly body on a windswept hilltop in the mountains of Virginia on a snowy day in December 1997. There were fifty white roses on top of his sky-blue casket, white because my mother's middle name means white rose, and fifty representing my parents' fifty years of marriage. As the snowflakes gently descended upon the old country graveyard, each flake seemed so appropriate since my father's last word was: "snow."

To mark his grave my mother asked our family to take a large rock from the stream behind her house. And on that rock my sister-in-law, Corrie, painted in simple letters: my father's name, the dates

of his life, a lovely snow-white edelweiss representing my parents' love of Switzerland where they often vacationed together, and the Scripture reference, John 3:16:

> *For God so loved the world that he gave his one and only Son, that whoever believes in him shall not perish but have eternal life. (NIV)*

That one verse sums up the great love my father discovered and which he sought so diligently to share with others.

If you would like to learn more about the love, hope and eternal life available in Jesus Christ I would love to hear from you. You may send an e-mail to will@willvaus.com or visit my web site: www.willvaus.com.

For now I leave you with a prayer ...

> *And I pray that you, being rooted and established in love, may have power, together with all the saints, to grasp how wide and long and high and deep is the love of Christ, and to know this love that surpasses knowledge—that you may be filled to the measure of all the fullness of God (Ephesians 3:17-19, NIV).*

NOTES

[1] Blaise Pascal, *Pensées*, trans. A. Krailsheimer, (New York: Penguin, 1966, revised edition, 1995), 148/428.

[2] Paul Gleye, *The Architecture of Los Angeles* (Los Angeles: The Knapp Press, 1981), p. 177.

[3] *Life: Mobsters and Gangsters*, Volume 2, No. 7, October 28, 2002, p. 115.

[4] Billy Graham, *Just As I Am* (New York: HarperCollins, 1997), p. 151.

[5] Public Domain.

[6] *Time*, April 25, 1955, p. 55.

[7] Alice Vaus, *Our Littlest Angel*, Tarrytown, New York, 1962, p. 4.

[8] Copyright 1954, by Singspiration, Inc.

[9] Youth Development, Inc., Articles of Incorporation, 1959.

[10] *Reaching the Unreachables, Time*, December 19, 1960.

[11] *Two-Man Attack On Harlem's Asphalt Jungle, Ebony*, June 1961, p. 27.

[12] *Reader's Digest*, Reprint, 1961.

[13] *The Wittenburg Door*, February-March 1971, p. 14.

Mary Haskett

REVEREND MOTHER'S DAUGHTER
A Real Life Story

In this gripping account, the author shares her personal story of racial rejection, physical and sexual abuse, and wartime trauma. Through it all, she is aware of a driving force in her life that ultimately brings her to Jesus Christ.

Terri Whitaker

YESUPADAM
Reaching India's Untouched

Yesupadam is the amazing story of God's miraculous work through an Untouchable Indian believer in Jesus and his Love-n-Care ministry in eastern India.

Fanny Goose
with Janet Fridman

RISING FROM THE HOLOCAUST
The Life of Fanny Goose

The astonishing real life story of an indomitable young Jewish girl who miraculously survives the horrors of Hitler's plot to destroy her people and goes on to live a joyful life.

www.BelieveBooks.com